ELEMENTS OF THE **EXTRAORDINARY**

Prophecies

Can you see into the future?

ELEMENTS OF THE **EXTRAORDINARY**

Prophecies

Can you see into the future?

GERALD BAILEY
Illustrated by Paul Fisher-Johnson

ELEMENT
CHILDREN'S BOOKS

SHAFTESBURY, DORSET · BOSTON, MASSACHUSETTS · MELBOURNE, VICTORIA

© Element Children's Books 1998
Text © Gerald Bailey 1998
Illustrations © Paul Fisher-Johnson 1998

First published in Great Britain in 1998 by
Element Children's Books, Shaftesbury, Dorset SP7 8BP

Published in the USA in 1998 by Element Books Inc.
PO Box 830, Boston MA

Published in Australia in 1998 by
Element Books Limited for Penguin Books Australia Ltd,
487 Maroondah Highway, Hardbacks, Ringwood, Victoria 3134

All rights reserved. No part of this publication may be reproduced or
transmitted or utilized in any form or by any means, electronic, mechanical,
photocopying or otherwise, without the prior permission of the Publisher.

The moral rights of the author and illustrator have been asserted.

British Library Cataloguing in Publication data available.
Library of Congress Cataloging in Publication data available.

ISBN 1 901881 40 7

Cover design by Ness Wood
Cover photography credits: BIBLE, MASK, RUNES, DIVINING BOWL –
by courtesy of Jon Stone; PYRAMID – by courtesy of Sue Thompson

Typeset by Dorchester Typesetting Group Ltd
Printed and bound in Great Britain by Creative Print and Design

Contents

Introduction		6
Chapter 1	What is Prophecy?	12
Chapter 2	The First Prophets	18
Chapter 3	Prophets and Kings	28
Chapter 4	The Old Techniques	31
Chapter 5	Prophets of the Bible	44
Chapter 6	Prophecy in Ancient Egypt	53
Chapter 7	Greek Prophets and the Oracles	63
Chapter 8	Merlin the Prophet	69
Chapter 9	Nostradamus	77
Chapter 10	The Prophecies of Nostradamus	82
Chapter 11	The Hitler Prophecy	90
Chapter 12	Revelations	98
Chapter 13	Prophets from Other Cultures	103
Chapter 14	Being a Prophet	108
Chapter 15	The Millennium Prophecies	114

Introduction

What is going to happen in the future? What wonderful, or perhaps horrible, events are going to take place? What is going to happen to me? Who will change the world for the better – or worse? People have been asking such questions for as long as questions have been asked. They are questions about the nature of the world in which we live, and about its many mysteries.

In trying to answer them we have created another world. A world of myth and of prophecy. Both tell the story of our universe and also that of its inhabitants, the supernatural powers, the gods, and the cycles of life. Myths explain how things came to be. Prophecy tells how things are going to be. It unlocks the door to the future. What a powerful gift prophecy can be, and little wonder that the prophets, the folk who unlock that door, have been at best feared and at worst put to death as witches for their troubles!

This book is about prophets and the mystery of prophecy. Prepare to be astounded!

The Great Prophet

It is said that a well-known prophet was given a test by his landlord, a certain Seigneur de Florinville. De Florinville asked the prophet to prophesy what would happen to two piglets that lived in the farmyard. The prophet frowned but answered that a wolf would eat the white one, while he and his landlord would eat the black one. In order to trick the prophet, de Florinville ordered his cook to kill the white one and roast it for supper that evening. However, as the piglet lay on the kitchen table ready for the oven, a young and curious wolf cub, kept as a pet in the household, hauled it on to the floor and began to make a meal of it. When the cook, who knew nothing of the trick, saw the mess, he immediately killed the other pig and served it for supper instead.

As they ate, de Florinville boasted to the prophet that he had disproved the prophecy about the pigs. But the prophet contradicted him, and so the cook was sent for. Looking rather sheepish, the cook admitted what had happened. The skeptical de Florinville was now convinced of the prophet's skill.

The prophet was the great Nostradamus, of whom we

shall learn more later. The prophecy of the pigs was not as earth-shattering in importance as many others that Nostradamus made, but it is still a form of prophecy. It involves looking into, and seeing, events that take place in the future or in a different time-plane. It also involves the alteration or heightening of the prophet's consciousness.

Beginnings

Prophecy probably began when man learned to think, even before the first great civilizations in the Mesopotamian valley and Egypt. It is difficult to locate the beginning of prophecy and its subsequent development, as you would perhaps with the science of physics. That's because it has always been a part of human society, regardless of its type. Prophecy is a kind of tradition, and early on its arts and disciplines were preserved in folklore, mythic tales, songs, and customs.

The first evidence that we have of prophecy comes from Mesopotamia, from the civilization that grew up between the Tigris and Euphrates rivers. One of its most famous cities was Babylon, which was well-known for its astrologers, some of whom, no doubt, were prophets in their own right. This does not mean that prophecy began in the time of Babylon, it simply means that this is where we have the first evidence of its existence. The Assyrians also studied the stars and formed the science of astrology. From here, we can find evidence of prophecy stretching to Egypt, Greece, Persia, India, the Far East, and China.

The first Babylonian texts deal with dream interpretation and the great creation myths with which prophecy is closely linked. These texts include wonderful poems, such as the *Epic of Gilgamesh*, in which the hero dreams of his enemies and then has the dream interpreted for him. Prophetic dreaming was developed to a high degree by the Greeks and Romans, who also involved themselves in magical sleep – special vision-creating meals and visions that took place at sacred sites.

Prophets who lived during the time of the Old Testament used dreams and dream interpretation a great deal in their prophecy, especially as astrology was considered evil and was therefore a forbidden art to them. Among the Jews of the Old Testament times, most dream interpretation became linked almost exclusively to the god known as Yahweh.

Prophecy was often associated with kings as well as priests and seers. From the Assyrians to the Celts in

Western Europe hundreds of years later, many mythic kings were empowered with the art of prophecy. In Eastern civilizations prophecy was very much part of the religious life of the people. In fact, Islam, one of the great world religions, was founded by the prophet Mohammed.

In Europe, during the late Middle Ages, interest in magic and divination seemed to grow more intense than ever. It was during this period that some of the greatest diviners and prophets lived, including Nostradamus. It was also a time of tremendous religious persecution, which meant that prophets had to be very careful about what they said and wrote. If not, they risked being accused of witchcraft and burnt alive at the stake!

Magic and prophecy became popular again in the nineteenth century, and even today it seems we are still intrigued by these mysteries. The interest shown by New Age groups, and even the advance of some scientific theories, has made many people more aware of the mystical – the spiritual traditions of images, energy, and consciousness – outside the purely material world of television, cars, and money.

And now, one momentous event looms large in all our futures, fuelling even greater interest in prophecy both past and present. It is the coming of the next Millennium. What are we to make of the prophecies relating to this wonderful event? What predictions did the fabulous Nostradamus make about the coming Millennium years? We shall soon see.

It seems that we will always be interested in what might happen to us, and to the world around us, whether that means poring over the astrology pages in the daily newspapers or practicing the arts of true prophecy. Perhaps the old ways are not so deeply buried beneath our modern collective consciousness after all.

CHAPTER 1

What is Prophecy?

What exactly is prophecy? It's not just about predicting a few events that might take place in the future. It's far more important and complex than that. In fact, two of the major religions of the world today, Christianity and Islam, have their roots firmly embedded in prophecy.

Nor is prophecy an outmoded superstition from the past. For instance, just consider the Stock Exchange, the weather, or the mighty computers that plot military strategy. They all involve some form of prediction or forecasting. Neither of these is true prophecy, but each shows our deep concern with the pattern and shape of events to come.

In order to make things a little simpler, let's divide the overall concept of prophecy into three categories:

What Is Prophecy? • 13

- ◆✦ Forecasting
- ◆✦ Prediction
- ◆✦ True prophecy

Forecasting is usually undertaken for the benefit of the individual. We want to know what will happen so we can make our plans in advance. If the weather forecast tells us it's going to rain, we don't go to Wimbledon or Flushing Meadow to watch the tennis. Prediction is more complicated and is undertaken for the benefit of people generally, although it can be abused and misused for personal gain. True prophecy, on the other hand, is selfless. It is concerned with events beyond the limits of the individual.

Our Consciousness

Prophecy requires a deeper or heightened consciousness – the prophet's mind has to enter a different state. This heightened consciousness allows the prophet to see the patterns and insights that those of us in a normal, conscious state do not see. Normal consciousness is when we are awake and making use of all our faculties, such as seeing, hearing, and smelling. Together, they give us a picture of the world around us. When someone punches us on the chin we get knocked out. We become unconscious and unaware of what is going on around us. When we fall asleep, we enter another layer of consciousness called the subconscious. It is full of thoughts and images that we sometimes remember as dreams.

The prophet reaches a higher, or altered, consciousness which allows him or her to see images and patterns that he or she would not ordinarily see. The trick is to find a path into this realm of altered consciousness, and this may be achieved in various ways, such as through meditation, fasting, or entering a trance. The patterns are there, all the time – but we have to find a means of seeing them. Even computers are now telling us that it is not always possible to predict a cause from an effect through simple logic. You have to see the pattern of things first. Human consciousness is sometimes able to see universal patterns, and these are the basis of prophecy.

Levels of Consciousness
Many ancient philosophers saw the universe as a type of music, with different levels of harmonies, octaves, and notes. Consciousness can be seen in the same way, with different levels blending into one another like the musical levels in a symphony, for instance. There are no hard barriers between the different levels. Forecasting, prediction, and prophecy can therefore be considered as three levels of consciousness, or three worlds, which blend into each other like the themes of a musical piece.

Forecasting involves the mind and emotions, the conscious and unconscious mind. Prediction reaches the soul and the solar world, while prophecy is the spiritual world of universal consciousness and insight. The prophet reaches his or her level of altered or expanded consciousness through the methods mentioned or perhaps through some other form of personal revelation, where future possibilities are revealed to him or her. The images and insights he or she receives may be revealed in different ways.

Receiving the Message
Prophets receive their insights and truths in different ways. Perhaps the purest form of prophecy comes when the prophet reaches a certain level of consciousness and is so motivated and excited that he or she is forced to utter in words the truth he or she sees or hears. The inspiration may come from the plane of consciousness he or she is on or from divine beings such as gods or heroes of the past. This is the rarest kind of prophecy and happened to

16 • **Prophecies**

Mohammad the prophet of Islam, Merlin, and others.

Prophets also gather knowledge from everyday observations, dreams, and images seen in trances. Sometimes the truths they acquire are important but sometimes they are quite ordinary, such as the prophecies in the ancient world regarding everyday things like the weather or the state of the crops.

Another method of receiving prophetic messages is through the study of certain signs, such as the flight of birds or the pattern of a set of animal bones, or through animal sacrifice. In this way simple objects are bestowed with a kind of mystical or divine energy. Many tales from ancient folklore recount this type of prophecy. Sometimes a tree or even a stone may be filled with magical energy which can inform the mind of a prophet who understands the signs.

Other messages are received through the direct voice of an entity from the other world, such as a divine being, or through the written word. The voice is heard physically through the ears. Such a voice often spoke prophetic words to the Hebrews of Old Testament times. Abraham, for instance, heard the voice of the Lord, and was in no doubt about who was talking to him. This kind of prophecy plays a large part in the development and formation of many religious beliefs, as we shall see later.

Written communication also comes from the other world, or from a god or goddess of some sort. The Book of Mormon is an example of a message written by a divine being that was used to forge a new religious group – in this case an offshoot of Christianity, the Church of Jesus Christ of Latter-day Saints, better known as the Mormon Church.

CHAPTER 2

The First Prophets

Over 5,000 years ago, between the Tigris and the Euphrates rivers in what is now Iraq, there existed a land called Mesopotamia. One of the world's first great civilizations grew up here, and along with it a succession of kings, priests and, of course, prophets. The prophets were mostly astrologers who lived in the fabulous city of Babylon, with its great hanging gardens and imposing ziggurats. These Babylonian astrologers studied the stars in great detail, and documented their movements and patterns with nothing but the naked eye. From these observations they developed an astrological system that helped them to interpret the future and predict what might come to pass.

The tradition of reading the stars probably came down to the Babylonians from ancient sources – possibly civilizations long dead, such as the lost kingdom of Atlantis.

Prophecy and similar arts may also develop within a society when it reaches a certain level of civilization. The prophets of Babylon probably benefited from both possibilities. At any rate, the Babylonians themselves believed that a king called Enmeduranki was the founder of the prophetic arts in Mesopotamia. He was a law-maker and a particularly gifted prophet who enjoyed interpreting dreams and symbols. Later prophets, who used the same methods as the king, came to be refered to as the Sons of Enmeduranki.

Some of the earliest Babylonian writing – written on clay tablets with slender, pointed instruments known as styli – was about dream interpretation. And this was often part of a long poem or epic. Robert Graves, the great 20th-century poet, believed that all fine poets work from some form of occult intuition. The most famous Babylonian epic poem is called the *Epic of Gilgamesh*, and it is still read today.

Gilgamesh

Gilgamesh lived long ago in the land of Mesopotamia. He was a mighty warrior and king, whose appetite for life was almost insatiable. His greatest desire was for conquest and he spent his life trying to fulfill that wish. This was all very well for the warrior, Gilgamesh, but his people soon became tired of his warlike ways. They begged the gods to deliver them from the brutal appetites of their king.

Then one night Gilgamesh had a dream. In it a terrible warrior, created by the gods, appeared and stood against him. It seemed that Gilgamesh had met his match.

When he woke up, Gilgamesh went to his mother, who

knew how to interpret dreams. She told him that the terrible warrior would indeed come and that his name was Enkidu. It was a prophecy that he must take seriously and act upon if he were not to be defeated by Enkidu. Gilgamesh learned from the prophecy and was able finally to withstand his enemy, after which they became friends. Through Enkidu and the prophecy, Gilgamesh's heroic energies were channeled in the proper direction and all ended well.

In ancient times dreaming was often seen as a means of interacting with the gods. The dream might be straightforward or it might be composed of images and symbols that meant little to the dreamer. These symbols had to be interpreted, and the prophet acted as the interpreter. He knew the true meaning of the symbols and images and could tell the dreamer what was going to happen. The prophets of ancient Babylon were adept at dream interpretation, and their skills were later passed on to the Greeks and Romans. Even Chinese prophecy might have been rooted in Babylonian tradition.

The Greeks and Romans

The Greeks and Romans took the art of prophetic dreaming to a very high level. They developed traditions which included magical sleep, finding special places to sleep where visions might appear, and even creating meals which, when eaten before sleep, induced prophetic dreams.

The Greeks were also extremely fond of oracles. An oracle, basically, is something that speaks to you. It might be at a shrine, an altar, a temple, or a grotto. The most famous oracle in Greece was, and still is, the oracle of Apollo at Delphi. Apollo was the god of prophecy as well as music and the arts. His oracle was a shrine where the priestess (usually an old, uneducated woman) known as the pythia became the voice of Apollo. He, through the pythia, prophesied what was to happen in certain situations.

The oracle of Zeus, another Greek god, is at a temple at Dodona. This is the oldest oracle in ancient Greece, but it was not as important as the oracle at Delphi. The oracle of Zeus was normally used to make decisions, such as who should be the next high official of Athens. Stones would be marked for each candidate and put into an urn or helmet at the temple. The helmet was then shaken until one stone jumped out. This would indicate the candidate chosen by

Zeus for the post.

The Romans, especially the Roman emperors, did not altogether like the idea of prophecy. They felt it was dangerous to their political lives. If, for instance, a sign prophesied their ultimate end it might be used against them by their enemies as an excuse for murder.

The Universal Compass

Nevertheless, the Romans did use prophetic techniques including oracles and a form of "universal compass." This universal compass – a sequence of circles along the horizontal and vertical planes to form links between cosmic directions, time, the seasons, and other things – was called a templum. The prophet, called an augur, used a curved wand to find a favorable place in the heavens, represented on the templum. Then he would specify which omens were to be looked for in that patch of sky and at what time. The omens might be a flock of birds, their calls, or a certain type of bird. If the favorable omen appeared then all would be well.

So now, if someone says to you, "That augurs well for the future," you'll know exactly what they are talking about, even if they don't!

The Sibyl

Prophets are generally considered to be superior to any other diviner. Prophecy is inspired and pure, or so thought the Greeks and Romans. The Romans considered the priestess of the god Apollo to be just such an inspired prophetess. She was called the sibyl. The sibyl's pronouncements, or Sibylline Prophecies, were collected in oracle books called Libri Sibyllini, which were consulted at times of trouble or natural disaster. However, as we know, the Roman rulers were afraid of the prophet's knowledge falling into enemy hands. So Augustus, the first Roman Emperor, outlawed any form of private divination and kept the Sibylline Prophecies for his own use. This way, if the prophecies said he was going to die at a certain time, no one could help that prophecy along by doing away with him and saying, "Oh, it's all right, I was just fulfilling the prophecy!" This is called using prophecy for propaganda purposes.

The Old Testament

The prophets that we know most about are described in the Christian Bible's Old Testament. Their prophecies came through hearing voices, reading symbols, and interpreting dreams. However, astrology and anything connected with magic was frowned upon, or even forbidden. Such matters were considered to be evil, or to be the work of the devil. In time, only dreams connected with the Jewish god Yahweh, and interpreted by his prophets, were thought to be truthful.

The prophets of the Old Testament lived about 4,000 years ago in the land of Canaan, later to become Judea and Israel. They included Enoch, Hosea, Daniel, Jeremiah, and Ezekiel. The most famous New Testament prophecies come from the Book of Revelations, which is a list of possibilities for the future, ending with some sort of terrible disaster. This is sometimes called "apocalyptic vision," and we'll talk more about it later.

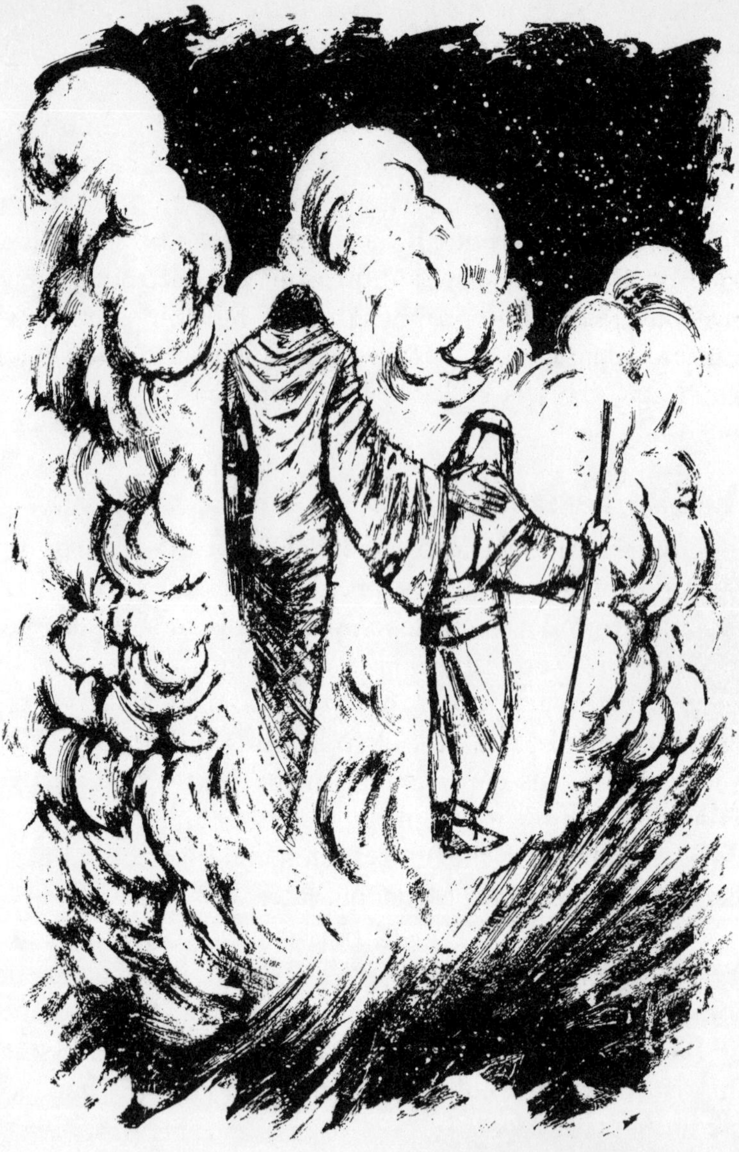

The Old Testament prophets sometimes forecasted disasters as well, but they also forecasted positive things, like the coming of a Messiah, a king, who would lead the Jews to freedom in their own land. This, of course, was the prophecy that heralded the birth of Jesus and later the rise of Christianity.

Usually, Old Testament prophets interpreted signs as the word of God, or heard the word of God in dreams. The prophet Enoch, however, did slightly better. Once, in a trance, he was able to leave his body and "walk with God." What he saw was not always encouraging:

> There I saw a place which had no firmament of the heaven above, and no firmly founded earth beneath it: there was no water upon it, and no birds, but it was a waste and horrible place.

Enoch was then told by an angel that the place he saw was the end of heaven and earth. Let's hope that Enoch's prophecy will not come about for a long, long time!

Oracles and Scribes

When prophets are in a trance or some other state of altered consciousness, they are not always able to write down what they have heard or seen. Ancient prophets might, therefore, need a scribe, or writer, close by to take down what they said. Sometimes the words or visions were not written down for some time after the prophecy had been made. Luckily, though, prophets generally had good memories and were able to pass on their prophecies by word of mouth, until someone finally wrote them down. People in times past had much better memories than we (essential in an age where information was not written down very often) and were used to the oral tradition. Many poems, such as the *Epic of Gilgamesh*, would have been memorized and spoken by the poet. The Celtic Irish developed a strong oral tradition as well, which was also associated with poetry and prophecy.

Still, it was always a good idea to write something down if possible, and so the scribe did the writing. Scribes, from Babylon and Assyria to later times, attended oracles and wrote down what the prophet said. We might think that, if they wanted to, they could write down more or less whatever they fancied. After all, the prophet, being in a trance, might never know the difference. But we have to accept that in most cases scribes took down exactly what they heard. Written accounts, such as the Sibylline Prophecies and the Prophecies of Merlin, were the result.

Merlin's Scribes

Legend tells us that the great magician Merlin, the friend and teacher of King Arthur, was also a marvelous prophet. He loved woodlands and observing the stars and planets, and these were the inspiration for his prophecies. However, the outdoors was not a place to be in winter, so his sister, Ganieda, fearful for his health, begged him to stay indoors during the harsh winter months. Merlin thought about this and wondered how he could stay indoors and still observe the heavens. The answer, he decided, was to build an observatory.

Merlin agreed to do as his sister suggested as long as she built him a house and the observatory he wanted. He also asked for servants to provide him with food and drink. However, as far as Merlin was concerned, the observatory was more important than the house. He specified that it had to have 70 doors and windows so he could watch the stars and the planets, because these would show him what was going to happen to the people of the kingdom. He also asked for the same number of scribes to take down and record the prophecies he made.

His sister dutifully built the house and observatory and, when winter came, Merlin lived in them even though he would have preferred to be outdoors. Here he became content to observe the stars and make many prophecies which the scribes wrote down.

CHAPTER 3

Prophets and Kings

Since ancient times, kings have often been both heads of state and heads of their particular religious group. Many have also been considered prophets in their own right. In Assyria, prophecy was linked with kingship, as it was in Babylonia. Often in these cultures, prophecies that were written down carried the name of the king in whose reign the prophecy was made. Prophecy might therefore be seen as a type of civic record-keeping.

Once it is connected with kings, prophecy must also be closely linked with the prosperity of the state or country. Prophecy often played an important role in the way a country was governed. Even the modern German dictator, Adolf Hitler, turned to forms of divination to justify his terrible goals and wanted to know what the future held, for fear of losing power.

In China, prophecy was an important guide for kings and leaders. The I Ching, The Book of Changes, was written as a manual for the personal guidance of kings and great men as well as ordinary citizens. It is the oldest prophetic system that has been in continual use in the world and it influenced the way kings behaved and acted in their role as rulers. It relies on sets of symbols to enlighten the prophet.

In Celtic Ireland, the king had a special relationship with the land he ruled. It is known as the divine wedding and meant that the king was symbolically a husband to the land and in tune with the goddess of the land. This relationship granted him inspiration and higher consciousness, the traditional spiritual state of a prophet.

Druid Prophets

In ancient Ireland, a sacred bull was brought forth to be sacrificed whenever it was time to chose a new king. The Druid priest who was in charge of the ceremony ate as much of the sacrificed bull as he could, until he was so full that he fell into a deep sleep. During his sleep certain incantations, or spells, were said over and over again. His subconscious mind reacted to the incantations and the priest began to receive revelations which told him who was the rightful heir to the throne. When he woke up, the Druid described his dreams and prophesied that a certain person would be king. In this way the new and rightful king was chosen.

Prophet at Ferns

A learned churchman called Gerald of Wales, who lived during the 12th century, was one of the first people to write a history of old Ireland. He told many fascinating stories of the "wonders and miracles" of the country he visited. One such story tells of the so-called Fanatic of Ferns, who "told the future from the past."

The fanatic in question was Fantasticus, a young man from the household at Ferns Castle. Apparently he plundered the church of St Maidoch, which was a bad idea because he immediately went into a frenzy and went mad. From that time on, led by some spirit or another, he began to prophesy. He said he could see the men of Ferns slain, and the castle laid low – he even mentioned names. He continued to prophesy day after day after day, which astonished everyone at the settlement. Then, just as the young man had predicted, an enemy attacked the castle and defeated the men of Ferns. Fantasticus did not stop prophesying until everything that he had foretold had come true and the castle of Ferns had been destroyed!

CHAPTER 4

The Old Techniques

In the dim and distant past, long before the coming of the great civilizations, religious duties were carried out by an individual called a shaman. Such people still exist today. The shaman uses animal helpers – usually a bird – to guide him into the other world, or world of spirits. He does this by going into a trance, brought on by drum-beat and dance. The journey, which he takes in an altered state of consciousness, brings him into contact with spirit guides who may give him advice, explain dreams, tell him how to heal a particular illness, or give him the power of prophecy.

Becoming a shaman is no easy business. He has to suffer terrible ordeals before he reaches his exalted state. His face is scoured with an abrasive substance to remove the old skin. This symbolizes rebirth. An Inuit shaman may have to spend five days immersed in freezing water, while sometimes a new shaman's body is inhabited by a dead shaman who proceeds to hack his body to shreds, causing untold agony. He sees all of this in a trance state. The aim of this initiation is to awaken the mind and harden the will, which elevates it above the trivialities of the day.

Shamans were perhaps the first prophets, even existing as far back as Cro-Magnon man, the first of our direct ancestors. But there is little proof of this, outside certain cave paintings that show men in animal masks. Still, it may be from these men that the prophets of the first civilizations learned their ways.

Siberia to the World

The shamans of Siberia, where the word "shaman" comes from, were less like witchdoctors or magicians, as was supposed, and more like mediums. The Manchurian word "samarambi" means "to excite oneself," while "samdambi" means "to dance." The Siberian shaman excites himself into a kind of ecstasy through drum-beating and dancing. Finally, he passes into a trance. At this point his spirit leaves his body. In his trance state he makes the sound of birds and animals and is thought to understand their language. Now he is able to use his powers to do different things including thought-reading, clairvoyance and, of course, prophecy. He is even able to discover thieves through the use of a mirror! The Siberian shaman also interprets dreams.

Shamanism spread from Siberia, in northern Russia, in all directions across the globe. It wended its way through Tibet and through China to Korea and Vietnam. Migrants

The Old Techniques · 33

took it across the Bering Strait to North America and from there to South America. Shamanism even exists in Africa and parts of Australasia.

In Europe there is a hint of shamanism in a very well-known figure – the witch on her broomstick. She may well have originated as a symbol of the ancient shaman in flight to the spirit world.

In Native American culture we often refer to the shaman as a witchdoctor. In fact, he performs all the tasks of the original shamans. Among the Plains Indians, the shaman would fast and go without sleep to attain an altered state of consciousness. Then he would make his spirit journey. Bunches of sage were burned in the hut to keep away evil spirits.

Shamans are still at work today. Some try to translate the old ways into a more modern form. Some doctors even work with shamanic ideas of self-healing to help patients. Helping and serving are what shamanism is all about. The shaman journeys on behalf of his client. His prophecies are not for him but for the one he serves.

Stones and Bones

Prophecy is often associated with different kinds of ritual or method. We have seen what the shamans go through to perfect their skills as well as what they do to achieve their altered state of consciousness. Some of the ancient methods are quite spiritual in nature, others are downright grisly – but they are equally effective to the prophet. They include prophecy by observation of bones and of other parts of the body!

The dead have always been important to ancient and traditional cultures. So it is not surprising that the bones of a dead person should be used as ritual objects. After all, bones represent death in a very literal way. Also, bones and skulls are an enduring reminder of a person whose spirit may still partially inhabit them. Bones, then, seem an obvious choice as a divining mechanism and as a method of prophecy.

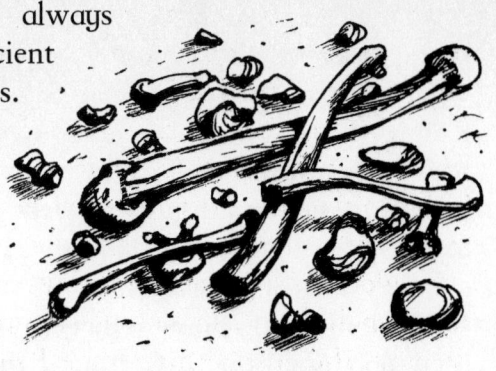

One way of using bones to prophesy at a child's birth is to find the name of an ancestor. The prophet holds the bones, says his invocation and recites the names of those in the spirit world who may want to join with the child's new life. If the correct name is given, the bones change weight in the prophet's hands.

The skulls of dead shamans were also used for prophecy. Sometimes they topped a wooden figure which was then questioned about the future. In Greek mythology, the priest Orpheus was dismembered, or torn to pieces. Afterwards his severed head became the mouthpiece of a prophet.

Divining with Animals

State prophets in Babylon practiced their art using the liver of a sheep. This gruesome-sounding method of divination is called hepatoscopy, and means using the interior organs of animals to gain prophetic insights. The liver was supposed to be the most important organ for divining. And it was used as such for thousands of years, right up to Roman times. This, of course, involved animal sacrifice, a practice we now consider barbaric and cruel. But we also have to remember that it was less cruel than battery-farming, seal-hunting, and many other modern ways of treating animals.

We don't really know why certain parts of the body were used and not others. Certainly the liver was thought to have some connection with the consciousness. Perhaps it is because some people consider animals to be more open to the unknown forces of nature, and so the future may more easily be imprinted on the liver of an animal than on that of a human.

Perhaps, also, it is part of the idea that there is a close link between natural patterns and prophecy. Diviners of the past not only looked at the internal organs of animals, they observed the patterns in which they moved, their individual shapes and the times at which they did things. These constituted omens from which patterns of the future might be understood. Other observations might also be made, using for example the swirling of smoke in the wind, the movement of water, or the flight of birds. All of these things might be prophetic omens.

Prophets of Dreams

As long ago as Babylonian times, prophets used dreams and the interpretation of dreams to make their prophecies. But what exactly did they see in their dream state or that of others? Again, prophets looked for omens and symbols. Like all signs, patterns, and omens, the ones seen in dreams may be guided by the unknown forces of the universe, the spirit world of the ancients. Some modern psychologists believe that many of the symbols we see are well-known in the subconscious minds of all people. These are called archetypes and they often form part of our dreams. Prophets are able to read dreams, which are sometimes visions of future events. Sometimes the dreams are straightforward, while at other times their meaning may be hidden in layers of symbols and signs. Sometimes prophets themselves dream and interpret. At other times they may interpret the dreams of the people they are helping. The biblical Joseph, for instance, interpreted the dreams of the Pharaoh, and these had monumental consequences for the Hebrews, as we shall see later.

Most traditional cultures knew the language of dreams, and dreams that foretold future events were considered to be quite normal. In ancient Babylon, prophets who interpreted dreams had to know about the symbols and patterns that were particularly important to their culture. The same was true for the prophets of ancient Egypt. Each was able to create an interpretation that connected people with their dreams. Shamans did, and still do, the same kind of thing.

The Dream World

Entering the dream world is like taking a walk into a strange new place full of shadows and unknown things. To get there you have to cross the threshold, or barrier, into the dream world. This barrier is partly constructed of fear.

Overcoming this helps you to prepare to make the crossing. The threshold is often seen as a dark door, a hole in the ground, or the entrance to a tomb. It leads into the shadows and into a world of what has sometimes been denied or repressed. To enter, you travel down into this underworld, the world of the unconscious mind.

Once there, you are in a place where dream events unfold and where different kinds of beings live and interact. All sorts of things, such as gods, souls, ghosts, previous lives, and important thoughts become real. It is a place that is at the same time real and imaginary. It is here, among these beings and events, that the dream takes place. Sometimes the structure of a dream may seem vague or meaningless. But at other times the patterns and events are clear, as if mapped out by some unknown force. These dreams may contain symbols and meaning that only a prophet might understand, or they might be clear enough for the dreamer to understand without help. The prophet experiences dreams that the unknown force has helped to create, and which give him a vision of some future event. Sometimes the dream answers a question. But, often, it is a warning!

Often dreams were written down. The Mesopotamian priests kept dream tablets on which dreams and their meanings were documented. These dreams were seen as direct messages from the gods. The Hebrew scriptures contain files of the dreams of the prophets – dreams which connected heaven and earth. Islam also has a rich tradition of dream writing and interpretation.

Natural Omens

Nature provided the ancient prophets with as many natural omens as they needed. But perhaps the most obvious were the flight patterns and movement of birds. The gift of this form of prophecy was thought to run in families. In ancient Greece, the prophet who read bird signs and had prophetic visions was called a mantis. Many ancient prophets believed that birds were messengers of fate, death, and transformation. They might also be spirit guides. In North America, the Hopi Indians dress as the spirit birds to ward off evil as well as to contact sacred spirits.

The owl and the vulture are associated with wisdom and with death. The dove symbolizes the holy spirit, while ravens, crows, and cranes can change shape – they are also associated with witches as familiars. In Greece at the time of the poet Homer, as well as in many other cultures of that period, the bird of omen was the lone eagle or hawk. It was called oinos and was associated with kings, destiny, blood, and sacrifice. The prophet knew the language of birds, just as the horse-whisperer knows the language of horses. This allowed him to see hidden patterns and so to visualize future events. Sometimes he saw birds as the physical appearance, or embodiment, of spirits, sometimes as spirit messengers. The skill of the prophet allowed him to interpret the signs and omens that the birds offered. Celtic Druids, for instance, would note the position and movement of ravens before making an important decision or taking a particular course of action. Some Celtic prophets even possessed their own divinatory birds. Taliesin, the

Celtic poet and prophet, was always accompanied by his eagle.

CROWS AND RAVENS

Of all the bird omens, crows and ravens seem to be the most interesting and the most ominous. Ravens, in particular, have become associated with evil – although that should not be the case because they can offer signs of positive events to come, or warn against actions that might lead to disaster or even death. In Tibet, ravens and crows were considered the best divinatory birds and their movements and cries were studied in detail. In modern times, during the Chinese takeover of Tibet, a Tibetan religious leader was met by a flock of crows as he and his party were fleeing from the country. He reported that while his party was making its way over a high mountain pass, a flock of crows appeared from an unfavorable direction and flew right at them in an attempt to turn them back along the pass. One even grabbed a horse's bridle and tried to pull the horse around. Unfortunately, the party of Tibetans did not heed the warning. In their rush to get out of the country they continued on their way, only to be met a short while later by a hostile band of Chinese soldiers looking for Tibetans on the run. The priest should not have ignored the warning!

Not long ago, while driving late at night along a country road, I noticed a small, light-colored object ahead of me. As I drew closer, the outline of the object became clearer. It was an owl standing in the middle of the road. In the headlights it looked as if it was glowing and I could see that it was clutching something in one claw. The owl did not move until I had pulled up alongside it. Then, it looked at me, turned, and flew off with a small rabbit in its grasp. I watched it until it had disappeared into the night, and thought no more of it. A few days later my car went off the road and hit a wall. Perhaps I should have been more careful after seeing the owl, an omen of misfortune and death!

THE PROPHET BULL

Prophets are usually human, but in ancient Egypt one prophet was not. He was a bull. But this bull was special. He was called the Apis bull and was thought to be the living image and representative of the god Osiris. There was only one Apis bull at a time, and when he died another one was chosen. The chosen bull was a lucky bull indeed, for he was treated better than most humans.

The Apis calf was first fed on rich milk at the place he was born. Then he was taken by scribes and prophets to the Egyptian city of Memphis. Here, he was given a fine place to live, with pleasure grounds and plenty of space in which to exercise. He was also provided with females, the most beautiful cows that could be found, to keep him company. They were kept in apartments where he could visit them whenever he wanted.

He drank from a fountain of pure water, because Nile water was considered too fattening for him!

The Apis bull did have some work to do, though. He was consulted as an oracle. When he was asked a question about the future, his movements were watched and from his actions omens were seen. Mostly he was offered some kind of food by hand. If he refused it, the omen was thought to be bad. The Egyptians also looked for omens about the state of the land according to the stable he happened to be in. It was a good omen if he chose to be in one stable, but a bad one if he chose to be in the other.

Once the unfortunate prince, Germanicus, offered the Apis bull something to eat. The bull looked at the food and sniffed it, then refused it. This was regrettable, and a bad omen. Sure enough, Germanicus died not long after.

CHAPTER 5

Prophets of the Bible

To Christians, the prophets of the Old Testament are probably the most important prophets of all, especially as they were responsible for prophesying the coming of the Messiah, or Christ, which we know as the coming of Jesus. Indeed, without the fulfilment of this prophecy there would be no Christianity as we know it. However, Hebrew prophets of the Old Testament prophesied far more than this.

The story of the Old Testament begins in Babylon, and we gain most of our information about it from what was written down at the time. In fact, Mesopotamia figures again in the story, because the patriarch Abraham migrated to Canaan from the Mesopotamian city of Ur. The first five books of Moses became the Hebrew Torah, or the Book of Law. Then the Book of the Prophets was added. This was important for the Hebrews as it strengthened their heritage, reinforcing the promise of Yahweh, their god, that a messiah, or anointed one, would come to lead the people to freedom. This story unfolds much later at Judea in the last few years BC where the Romans, under the famous general, Julius Caesar, had taken over the country. They later appointed Herod as King of Judea. His was a harsh rule indeed, and it was into this environment that Jesus the Nazarene was born. Was he the Messiah, the anointed one, of the prophecy? We shall see.

The prophecies of Moses were contained in what are called the five books of the Pentateuch – Genesis, Exodus, Leviticus, Numbers, and Deuteronomy. The major prophets who came after Moses were Joshua, Isaiah, Jeremiah, Ezekiel, and Daniel. Their work is recorded in the Books of the Prophets, which were written by or about the Hebrew prophets and named after them. There were many other minor prophets as well.

Professional and Classical Prophets

In Old Testament times, the Hebrews of ancient Palestine produced two types of prophet – professional and classical. Professional prophets earned a living by trying to work out for their clients how God felt about the particular problems or decisions that they had to face.

Classical prophets did not choose to become prophets. They believed that they had been called by God to deliver His message to the Hebrew people. Sometimes these prophets are called literary prophets because their words were written down. In some cases, prophecies were made in the form of poems, which are now considered works of great literature as well as works of spiritual value.

ISAIAH

Isaiah is the longest of the Books of Prophets in the Old Testament and was probably written by more than one person between the 8th and 6th centuries BC. The first 39 chapters, which are often called First Isaiah, contain the prophecies of Isaiah of Judah. He lived during the reign of King Hezekiah in the 8th century BC.

Isaiah's prophecies told the Hebrews that, if they were to prosper, they must have faith and trust only in Jehovah, their God. They must not become involved in political or military actions. Furthermore, Jehovah's powers were not limited to the Hebrews – which meant he could punish their enemies if he so wished.

The Second Isaiah was probably written during the period in which the Hebrews were held captive in Babylonia. This began after the destruction of Jerusalem in 587 BC. The main prophecies said that the Hebrews would return to their home in Judah in 538 BC. This was very important for the Hebrews, as it kept their morale high. And, just as the prophet predicted, the Hebrews were indeed returned to their homeland during that very year.

Most importantly, though, Isaiah prophesied the birth of the Messiah, the anointed one. This prophecy, contained in chapter 9, verses 1 to 7, shifted the emphasis of his prophecies to a period further into the future, and predicted the New Covenant, or the agreement that Yahweh, the Hebrew's God, had with his chosen people. It would not be until six centuries later that the Messiah appeared as Isaiah had foretold.

EZEKIEL

In order to understand the importance of the Hebrew prophets in the Old Testament we need to know something of the history of that time in Palestine, around the 8th to 6th centuries BC. The most powerful nations in the Near East were Assyria and Babylonia to the north in Mesopotamia, and Egypt to the south. Palestine, or Canaan, was caught in the middle of these two mighty powers and was divided into Israel and Judah. Israel was already under the domination of the Assyrians, while Judah tried to remain independent. The prophets had much to say about the situation. Or, rather, Yahweh did, because He spoke to His people, the Hebrews, through His prophets. The prophets were called to their position by Yahweh. They did not have any choice in the matter, either, and became prophets whether they liked it or not. Some did not.

When the power of Assyria declined, the might of Babylon grew, particularly under its great king, Nebuchadnezzar. Ezekiel prophesied that Jerusalem would be destroyed by Nebuchadnezzar, and for this he was disliked. Some Hebrews thought they could resist Babylon, that Yahweh would protect them. But Ezekiel let them know that Yahweh was not pleased with the Hebrews. Even though they were His chosen people they had descended into idol worship and immorality, following the gods of the Babylonians and others. For this Yahweh intended to punish them and He was going to use Nebuchadnezzar as His weapon.

Then the Hebrews looked to Egypt for help against Babylon, which made Yahweh even angrier. The Hebrews should at least have trusted to their own god for help.

Ezekiel, the prophet, spoke of the destruction to come. He even acted out the situation to try to impress the Hebrews. In one instance he illustrated a tile with a drawing of a siege machine propped against the walls of Jerusalem. Then he acted out the consequences of exile by eating only sparingly and carrying the pack of an exile. None of this did much good. He complained that the people only came to him to be entertained and did not act on his advice.

All was not lost, however, as Ezekiel also prophesied that after the exile the Hebrews would be returned to their land and that Israel and Judah would be united under one king. Peace and "unprecedented" fertility would follow. But first the Hebrews had to be punished, and they duly were. Jerusalem fell to Nebuchadnezzar in 587 BC. Many Hebrews, including their leaders, were sent into exile in Babylon where they remained for 70 years.

Ezekiel spoke many prophecies against the neighboring countries of the Hebrews as well as against his own people. God's voice in him said that those who had abandoned Judah would also be punished. Needless to say, Nebuchadnezzar conquered all of the surrounding countries and gained control over that whole area of the Near East.

Regardless of what they called "the spirit that moved them," the Old Testament prophets seemed to get most things right. Perhaps they were simply very aware of the political situation in their part of the world and could easily see things coming. Or perhaps they were, indeed, inspired by the word of a higher consciousness.

JEREMIAH

Jeremiah was another Hebrew prophet who lived during the 7th century BC. He certainly didn't want to be a prophet. However, he said that he could not contain God's anger at the Hebrews, so he had no choice and was called to writing everything down. Yahweh, the Hebrew God, said to him: "Commit to writing all the words I have spoken to you, for days are coming when I shall restore the fortunes of my people." In fact, Jeremiah used a secretary called Baruch to do much of the writing. Jeremiah prophesied under five kings of Judah, and was very young when he was called by Yahweh to be His voice and His scribe.

Jeremiah knew the power of Nebuchadnezzar, as Ezekiel had done, and knew that the Hebrews had no chance against such a ruthless king. "The kings of the north would come and set their thrones at Jerusalem's gates," were the words he used in the prophecy. He made it clear that he thought Judah should submit to Babylon as there was no point in fighting. This attitude did not please the Hebrew leaders, who persecuted Jeremiah for voicing his prophecies. At one point he was thrown into a disused cistern and left to die, only to be rescued by a friend before he perished.

Jeremiah continued to prophesy, forecasting that the Egyptians, who could have helped the Hebrews, would be annihilated by Nebuchadnezzar's armies. He was proved right when the Babylonian king swept aside an Egyptian army at the battle of Carchemish in 605 BC.

The Messianic Prophecy

When Jeremiah finished prophesying about the fall of

Judah and the exile to Babylon, he began to prophesy about the return of the Hebrew people to the promised land of Judah, their home, and of a new relationship with Yahweh, their God. This new relationship was to be seen as the New Covenant, or agreement, with Yahweh. He had already made one with the Hebrews, through Moses, but it had obviously not worked because the Hebrews had not kept their part of the bargain. So now He proposed a new one. This time it was to be a covenant between Yahweh and each individual Hebrew. It would ultimately be fulfilled with the coming of the Christ and His gospel – in fact, the coming of Yahweh himself to work among the people. This is a kind of follow-up to the words of Isaiah, which tell of the birth of a special individual referred to as the "Messiah." A messiah is the anointed one, or the king – messiah means "anointed one" in Hebrew. This is the single most important prophecy to Christians, who accept that Jesus, the Nazarene, was indeed the Messiah. The Hebrews, or Jews, do not agree with this – they are still waiting for the prophecy to be fulfilled.

Still, before the coming of Jesus, the prophecies remained an important part of the Hebrew religion and showed that Yahweh had not deserted His people, even though he had dealt out some pretty strong punishment when they had gone against His wishes and worshiped other gods. The prophecy also ensured that the Temple of Solomon and the Wall of Jerusalem were rebuilt.

The Old Testament stories end around the 4th century BC, and we have to wait for another 300 years, until the last years of the final century BC, before the threads of the story are picked up again. At this point, the great power in the world was Rome and, in 63 BC, Roman legions marched into Palestine under the leadership of Julius Caesar.

At this point, Palestine was made up of three separate provinces – Galilee in the north, Judea in the south, and Samaria squeezed in between. Caesar had appointed a man called Antipater to be the ruler of Judea, and Herod, his son, was the governor of Galilee. Antipater was killed soon afterwards, and so Herod was made King of Judea. Most people saw Herod as a usurper. He did not come from the line of kings who had ruled Palestine since the days of Solomon and David. Moreover, he was a cruel, despotic character who levied high taxes and crucified around 3,000 people to make sure the Hebrews submitted to Rome.

Once again, the Hebrews were oppressed and in need of help. They wanted their messiah, a strong leader who would liberate them from the hated Romans. Into this environment was born Jesus, a Nazarene. We do not know for certain, but it is probable that Jesus was a descendant of the old Hebrew kings, and so came from the line of David. This would certainly make him an "anointed one," a potential king, and in the Greek, "Christ." Contrary to popular belief, He was not a carpenter – the Hebrew word that is often translated as "carpenter" actually means "master" or "scholar." At any rate, it was this Jesus who became the leader who would free the Hebrews, or Jews, from the Romans.

Unfortunately, not all of the Jews were behind Him. Jesus wanted to help all people regardless of their background, and nationalist Jews objected to this. Finally, Jesus was betrayed by some of His own people, was handed over to the Romans, and was crucified – or so we are led to believe. The most important point, though, is that He made enough impact to be regarded as the Messiah and to convince many people that He could be seen as the true light and symbol of a new way. This led to the development of a religion which uses the word Christ as its core. We call that religion Christianity. Is this what the prophets of the Old Testament really saw?

CHAPTER 6

Prophecy in Ancient Egypt

When Joseph, the son of Jacob, was sold into slavery in Egypt around 1420 BC, he probably had little idea what was in store for him. A life of hardship and grueling physical labor was usually the lot of Egypt's slaves. But Joseph had a gift. And this gift served him well. It also changed the course of Jewish history.

Joseph's Amazing Technicolor Dreams

When he was young, Joseph had two strange dreams. In the first he dreamed that he and his 11 brothers were cutting sheaves of corn in a field. Suddenly, his sheaf stood upright and those of his brothers bowed to it. In the second dream, the sun, the moon and 11 stars all bowed to him. These dreams were interpreted to mean that Joseph's family were acknowledging him as their lord. Needless to say, his 11 brothers were not pleased about this. Eventually, to make sure the dream did not come true, they decided to kill Joseph. However, they thought better of it and decided to sell him to a passing band of traders on their way to Egypt. He was sold for 12 shekels of silver, although the brothers told Jacob, their father, that Joseph had been devoured by a wild animal.

In Egypt, the traders sold Joseph to Potiphar, the Pharaoh's captain of the guard. Joseph was a faithful and good servant, but he got on the wrong side of Potiphar's wife, who unjustly accused him of attacking her, and ended up in jail. There, Joseph came upon both the Pharaoh's cup-bearer and his baker, both of whom had upset the Pharaoh. One morning both were found looking downcast after having disturbing dreams. No one could interpret them, until Joseph asked what the matter was. He immediately interpreted both dreams. He told the cup-bearer that he would soon be restored to his position, but the baker, he said, would fare badly and be beheaded! Both interpretations came true. The cup-bearer said nothing about this to his master, and it was not until two years later that Joseph was again asked to interpret a dream.

This time it was the Pharaoh himself who could find no one to interpret his dream. The cupbearer, who remembered Joseph's success, suggested that the Pharaoh should seek help from the Hebrew. The Pharaoh at once sent for Joseph and told him that no one could interpret his dream. Joseph answered that he could not do it either, but that God would provide the answer.

The Pharaoh then told him about the dream. He was standing on the bank of the Nile when out of the river came seven cows, fat and sleek, and they grazed among the reeds. After them appeared seven other cows – scrawny, gaunt, and lean. These ate up the seven fat ones, yet they remained as gaunt and skinny as before. Then the Pharaoh said that he saw seven ears of corn, full and good, growing on a single stalk. After that, seven others appeared – withered, thin, and blighted by the wind. The thin ears swallowed up the seven good ears.

Joseph said that the dreams were one and the same. God had told Pharaoh what He was about to do. The seven good cows were seven years and the seven good ears of corn were also seven years. The same applied to the seven gaunt cows and the blighted ears of corn. Seven years of plenty were coming to Egypt, but seven years of famine would follow. Then all the abundance of Egypt would be forgotten and the famine would ravage the land. Joseph told the Pharaoh to appoint a wise man, a commissioner, to look after the land. He should take one-fifth of the harvest from each good year and store up the grain ready for the famine years.

The Pharaoh decided that there was no one wiser and shrewder than Joseph, so he made him the commissioner. In fact, he made Joseph second-in-command only to the Pharaoh himself.

In time, the prophecy proved true and the Pharaoh invited all of Joseph's family to join him. He did this after reprimanding them and forgiving them for what they had done to Joseph.

Needless to say, Joseph's father, Jacob, was more than a little surprised to see his son alive, let alone second-in-command of mighty Egypt. Joseph settled his family in the land known as Goshen in northern Egypt, and they remained there for many years.

Yuya

The story of the prophecy and the Hebrews moving into Egypt is an interesting one, but it does not exist in Egyptian history, which is strange indeed for such a supposedly monumental episode. The exodus of the Hebrews out of Egypt under Moses is also not documented. But some scholars may have an explanation for this. They believe that a man called Yuya, whose mummy is preserved in the Cairo Museum, was the real Joseph. The mummy even has features that are more Hebrew than Egyptian.

We know a lot about Yuya, and his story parallels that of the biblical Joseph. Except for one thing. It is generally believed that Joseph went to Egypt in the early 1700s BC where the Hebrews lived for 300 years, whereas Yuya lived during the 1400s BC, which would mean the Hebrews were in Egypt for a much shorter length of time. The Pharaoh who appointed him to the post of commissioner, or vizier, was Tuthmosis IV. Yuya served Tuthmosis and then Amenhotep III when he succeeded to the throne. Amenhotep married Yuya's daughter, Tiye.

One problem with placing the descent of the Hebrews into Egypt in the late 1700s BC is chariots. Strange as this may seem, chariots do make a difference. They are mentioned three times in the Old Testament story of Joseph. Yet no chariots were used for warfare in the late 1700s BC. They came into use probably during the next century, but were certainly there during the life of Yuya.

Another problem with the normal chronology is that slavery, of the type Joseph was sold into, did not become common in Egypt until the 18th dynasty of the Pharaohs, which was not until after the 1700s BC.

Tuthmosis IV was known as a dreamer. An inscription on a sphinx tells of one of his inspired dreams. He would certainly have thought highly of a man who could rightly interpret them. And this man must have been Joseph, known as Yuya.

There are many other reasons to suppose that Joseph was in Egypt much later than most historians think. And from this we have to accept that the stay of the Hebrews in

Egypt was not 400 years, as the Bible writers say, but just a few generations. If this is the case, then we must assume that Joseph, or Yuya, really did live and was, indeed, the Pharaoh's vizier – as well as a highly gifted prophet.

The Prophecy of the Pyramids

For thousands of years one huge building has caused scientists and other observers to gasp in admiration, and sometimes in disbelief. It is the Great Pyramid, one of the seven wonders of the ancient world. How could such a monument have been built so many years ago, and how long must the job have taken? Most students of Egypt, known as Egyptologists, believe it was built as a tomb at the time of the Pharaoh Khufu, also known as Cheops. He reigned during the Old Kingdom period of Egypt from 2589-2566 BC. Others, though, believe that the pyramid could not have been built during one man's lifetime and that it was most likely built thousands of years before as a center for learning. The people who built it, they claim, may have been the descendants of the lost kingdom of Atlantis, a legendary island believed to be submerged beneath the Atlantic Ocean.

Most likely, the Great Pyramid was built as a tomb for Khufu by Hemon, the chief of works. It took 20 years to build and cost £5 million in silver. No one is sure exactly how it was built but its measurements and shape have apparently revealed some startling information, not least some astounding prophecies.

It is the geometry of the pyramid and its interior vaults and passages that are so important. They prophesy the history of humanity from beginning to end. This theory was chronicled in 1925 by David Davidson, a structural engineer who had studied the Great Pyramid for 24 years. He found a system of prophetic dates that spanned 6,000 years, beginning in 3999 BC and ending in AD 2001. The dates came from the mathematics of the pyramid's astronomical alignment and its geometry. Davidson even found symbolic meaning in the types of stone used, their alignment, and their coloring.

The ratio of one pyramidal inch to one year is the basis for the time-scale, and historical events have apparently confirmed the accuracy of this scale. For instance, the ascending passage known as the Hall of Truth in Darkness begins with the date 1486 BC, and this is supposedly the time of the Hebrew exodus from Egypt. Where the passage opens up into a larger vault is reckoned at 4 BC, the birth date of Christ. Another passage begins at 1939 and ends at 1953. The first date indicates the start of World War II, while the second is significant as the end of a number of events from the war to the hydrogen bomb. It is also a significant date in the Mayan Indian calendar cycle, and we will learn more about this later. The passage between the antechamber leading to the king's chamber and the chamber itself has two very significant dates at the beginning and end. The first is August 4-5, 1914, the beginning of World War I, and the second is November 11, 1918, when it ended. If Davidson and others are correct, then the Great Pyramid and its builders made some very accurate prophecies of world history so far. And they would certainly lead us to see the passage of time and space in a quite different light. From this, we might assume that further dates noted on the Pyramid make predictions about the time leading to the year 2000, the Millennium, and beyond. They do. But we'll deal with these in the Millennium Prophecies chapter.

The Mummy's Curse

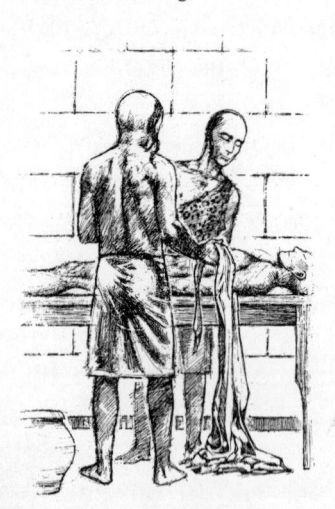

The ancient Egyptians believed very much in an afterlife, and that the body of a dead person should be left intact in order to help the person enter into that next life. The body was preserved for the future through a process called mummification. This involved removing the soft contents of the abdomen and the brain, then soaking the body in natron, a mineral, to dry it out. Finally, the body was wrapped in bandages and sealed with resin. The result was a mummy!

When the Arabs arrived in Egypt in the 7th century AD, they did not entirely understand the old ways of Egypt and were fearful of them. They called the country by its old name, Keme, and anything to do with its ancient mysteries were called "al Keme," or "the Egyptian matter." From this we get the word "alchemy." The Arabs believed that by saying the right spells they could make invisible things, hidden by the ancients, appear. They also believed that the ancients, preserved as mummies, would do anything to protect their belongings, including prophesying the death of anyone who despoiled their tomb. This became known as the Mummy's curse.

George Herbert, Earl of Carnarvon, was an enthusiastic amateur archaeologist. But, most importantly, he was the sponsor of Howard Carter, the man who found the tomb of Tutankhamun. As a man of science, Carnarvon probably thought little of the stories of curses which surrounded mummies. So he entered the tomb of Tutankhamun with Carter in 1923.

In March of that year a novelist called Marie Corelli wrote to the *New York Times* that she had in her possession one of the earliest Arabic books concerned with the opening of Egyptian tombs. And in it there was a passage which read: "Death comes on wings to him who enters the tomb of a pharaoh." Corelli then prophesied the deaths of all those working on the tomb.

The article might have been forgotten, had not Carnarvon died just two days later! Apparently a mosquito bite, which he had received in Egypt, had become infected. This led to pneumonia, from which he later died. Death had certainly come on wings, and the story made headline news all over the world.

The Divining Bowl

The divining bowl, or scrying bowl, is a method of seeing and gaining inspiration by using water as a mirror. It has been used by many cultures and is associated with different deities, or gods, such as the Greek goddess Demeter, and Metis, the goddess of shifting water. In Egyptian myth, the divining bowl is associated with Anubis, the jackal-headed god of the dead. He weighed the heart of a dead person against the Feather of Truth.

Nectanbo, an Egyptian prince of the 4th century BC, created magic using a bowl of water, an ebony rod, and wax figures. He would put the wax figures, which represented enemy soldiers and their ships, into the water of the bowl, recite spells, and touch the wax figures with the rod. They would then come to life and quickly sink to the bottom of the bowl. His real enemies would be destroyed at the same time.

The vision concept of the bowl is that it shows a way into other worlds. If you throw melted wax into it, you can read the symbols made by the wax as it dances on the water. Lead and hot oil can also yield shapes that can be interpreted.

CHAPTER 7

Greek Prophets and the Oracles

Ancient Greece and other parts of the Mediterranean possessed many shrines where oracles told of the future.

The Oracle at Delphi

However, none was more important than the shrine at Delphi, established for the god Apollo. People would come from all over the ancient world to hear the words of Apollo's priestess, the pythia, who acted as the voice of the great god of prophecy, music, and the arts. All kinds of people came as well, including statesmen, religious leaders, poets, philosophers, and ordinary citizens.

To consult the oracle at Delphi, you had to climb the heights to the sacred site, which was a particularly stunning place. The best time to visit was the seventh day of the Greek month Byzious – February and March – when many pilgrims would throng the sacred way leading to the shrine. As you entered the antechamber, birds flew from around the many statues which filled it, causing a rush of air. Then the priest called out for the pure at heart to approach and you would walk down a long, statue-lined colonnade carrying an offering of honey cakes and an animal sacrifice. Huge doors made of wood and ivory swung open at the end, and at the bottom of the inner room stood the altar, bathed in light. Beneath it was the entrance to the grotto where the prophecies were made.

Once inside, the animal sacrifice was burned, then the pythia, Apollo's priestess, would enter. She was usually an old woman dressed in white and crowned with a laurel wreath. She received the name "pythia" from the gigantic female python, who was also a prophetess, that Apollo had to kill in order to establish his shrine in that particular place. The pythia descended into the grotto, while throwing grain and laurel leaves into the fire, and took her place on the sacred tripod. You followed her down, where you saw a huge laurel tree and a stone with the words "navel of the world" written on it. There were also statues of Apollo and Dionysus in gold looking down upon you. Finally, the pythia went into a trance and you smelt a sweet scent. It was now time to ask the priestess a question. She would answer in a rather ghostly voice and your consultation was over.

Alexander and the Oracle

Alexander the Great, King of Macedonia, was one of the greatest generals the world has ever known. But even he, a man who conquered most of the known world, sought advice from an oracle. He knew the importance of reaching beyond the ordinary consciousness of everyday life to look for direction elsewhere – from a more universal power.

Alexander was just 20 years old when he began his attack on the crumbling Persian empire. He marched and fought southwards for many months, through Asia Minor and the lands on the eastern shore of the Mediterranean, until he finally defeated the Persians at Issus in 333 BC. He entered Egypt the following year.

Alexander was greeted there as a king and a savior. He made sacrifices to the proper gods, especially the Apis bull, which went down very well, because the Persians had slaughtered the Apis bulls when they had entered Egypt. He acted publicly as King of Egypt and was accepted by both the priests and the people.

The following year Alexander visited a place on the Nile Delta called Rhacotis. He liked the high ground that it was on and, after exploring the area further, decided that this was the place to found a new city. He personally laid out the boundary of the place using pearls of barley. This was important as it was thought that when birds flew down and pecked the barley, prophets prophesied the coming of many citizens and prosperity for the city. Aristander, the prophet, said the city would certainly prosper, especially from the fruits of the earth. And it did – that city was, of course, Alexandria, which is still a major Egyptian city.

The Oracle at Siwa

After founding Alexandria, the new Egyptian king had an urge to visit the oracle at Siwa. We can only guess at his reason, because he never said what it was. Nevertheless, he began his journey along the coast through fairly hospitable desert to Paraetonium. After that, the going was much harder, with dust storms and lack of water. But Alexander need not have worried. Two crows appeared and led him and his party through the desert to their destination, the oasis of Siwa. Once again we see the importance of crows as omens and guides.

On their arrival at Siwa, Alexander's companions were ordered by the priest of the oracle to change their clothes before approaching. Alexander, however, was sent, without having to change his clothes, into the inner sanctum. The others were told to stay outside. The King was allowed in to hear the prophecy of the oracle, which was expressed through nods of the head and signs rather than words. The priest greeted Alexander as the "son of Zeus" (the supreme god of the ancient Greeks). Strangely, no one knows what Alexander asked the oracle. He told no one, and only said that the answers pleased him. Most scholars believe, though, that Alexander wanted to be assured that he was the son of Amon, the Egyptian form of Zeus, and that this was very important to him. In any event, the encounter with the oracle seemed to make a great impression on him.

Some months later, an envoy from Greece said that an oracle that had remained silent since the Persian occupation had spoken and confirmed Alexander's relationship to Amon, as well as forecasting his future. At the same time the Sibyl of Erithrea on the mainland coast opposite Chios affirmed his "exalted birth."

Alexander went on to conquer lands as far east as India.

Teiresias, the Seer

One of the most mysterious prophets of ancient Greece was the seer Teiresias. He was able to speak the language of birds and snakes. He was blinded and yet was given the gift of "sight" by the goddess Athena. It was also believed that he could be both man and woman while living for as long as seven generations. He was possessed of a far-reaching consciousness that could pass from one form of reality to another, allowing him to see the future and consult with the spirit world.

The Greek hero, Odysseus, came upon Teiresias in the underworld, also called Hades. Teiresias was able to show

Odysseus the way to return home. It was also Teiresias who, in the stories of Oedipus, revealed to the prince that he had killed his father and was married to his own mother. So Teiresias brought both good fortune and bad.

CHAPTER 8

Merlin the Prophet

The young man looked at the weatherbeaten face and muscular arms of the Saxon King, Vortigern. This King had power indeed, and he intended to use it to sacrifice the youth in order to maintain the crumbling tower that stood in front of them. Vortigern intended to use magic to get his way. But the young man had other ideas. He knew the tower, and begged Vortigern for a chance to speak.

Vortigern agreed and the youth told him about the tower. Underneath it, there was to be found a cave, and in that cave a pool. In the pool lay two

70 • **Prophecies**

dragons asleep. The Saxon King was intrigued.

So Vortigern and the young man, whose name was Merlin, descended into the cave. Vortigern ordered that the pool be drained, and at that point the two dragons awoke and confronted them. Merlin burst into tears, which was a sign, and began to utter prophecies.

This is the symbolic story of how Merlin came to be

filled with energies bursting from beneath the earth. The cave, the pool, and the dragon all aroused the powers of prophecy in him, the powers to lock into the mystical otherworld forces and to see into the future.

Of all the Celtic prophets, the best-known by far is the great Merlin. Most people know him as the strange figure who befriended the boy Arthur in the legends of the Round

Table and the Holy Grail. But Merlin was more than that. Like all prophets before and after, Merlin was able to tune into the basic mythology and history of all things, from beginning to end – rather like seeing the beginning and end of the universe as a picture book which the prophet can open at any page, given the right help.

Legend has it that Merlin, whose full name was Merlin Ambrosius, was born in the Welsh town of Carmarthen. His mother was a princess but his father was said to be a dark and shadowy figure, probably a demon. From him Merlin inherited his magical and prophetic powers. His prowess as a prophet was considered so great by medieval Europeans that it was included in the index of the Council of Trent, the periodic meetings of Roman Catholic churchmen held in 16th-century Italy.

Merlin was a true Celt or Briton, and lived during the time of the Saxon invasions of Britain. Vortigern ruled over the areas of Britain that the Saxons had conquered. He obviously knew of Merlin's powers and called the prophet before him. Merlin fell into a trance and spoke many more prophecies than the Celts could recall. But this much was remembered – he prophesied the coming of a mighty British ruler who was symbolized by the Boar of Cornwall. He also prophesied that Aurelius Ambrosius and Uther, the rightful princes to the throne of Britain, would return and overthrow Vortigern. Sure enough, they landed at Totnes and marched against the Saxon. Vortigern withdrew to the castle at Genareu but, after a siege, he was captured and burned to death.

Another story tells of Aurelius defeating Hengist, the

Saxon leader, after he had brutally killed many noble Britons. Aurelius decided to erect a monument on Salisbury Plain to honor the nobles who had been massacred, and asked Merlin for his help. Merlin took Aurelius to a circle of stones in Ireland, which they both agreed would make a splendid monument. Merlin then used his magical powers to dismantle the stone circle, after which it was shipped back to England. It is still there today, and we know it as Stonehenge.

Unfortunately for Aurelius, Merlin soon prophesied his death. Aurelius was lying ill in the West Country when a freshwater pool that supplied his drinking water was poisoned by the Saxons. He died of the poison and his brother Uther, who took the title Pendragon, became leader of the Britons. It was through Uther that the prophecy of the great Briton leader came about.

The Birth of King Arthur

Uther invited the King of Cornwall to a banquet, and before long he fell in love with the King's wife, Igraine. The Cornish King was not happy about this. He quickly left the gathering with his wife and returned to his castle at Tintagel. Uther considered the quick departure to be an insult and laid siege to the Cornish castle, but without much luck. Again he turned to Merlin who, using his mystical powers, made Uther look just like the Cornish King. In this changed shape, Uther was able to enter Tintagel unopposed and spent the night with Igraine. On the same night the King of Cornwall was slain in battle and later Uther married Igraine. The result was the child, Arthur, whose upbringing was overseen by Merlin until his time of destiny was due.

Unfortunately, Merlin did not always use his powers wisely. He fell in love with Nineve, the daughter of a Sicilian siren, and taught her all the magic he knew. In time, she learned so much that she was able to put the great magician himself under a spell that trapped him forever in an enchanted wood. "I am the greatest fool," he told the knight Gawain who once passed by him, "I loved another more than I loved myself."

The Real Merlin

The life of Merlin is shrouded in the mists of legend and folklore. But he may well have been based on an historical person who lived in the 6th century. This was Lailoken, a Briton who had become crazed as a result of a battle in Cumbria. From then on he wandered about the forests of Britain, an inspired madman. The Welsh called him Myrddin and believed that, among other things, he had prophesied the rise of the Welsh as a strong nation once again.

The person who linked Merlin to the story of Arthur was a writer of the 12th century, Geoffrey of Monmouth. This Norman lord documented the prophecies of Merlin in a verse biography called *The Vita Merlini*, which was written mostly in Latin, with some Old Welsh thrown in. The book contains much Celtic lore and was probably put together using the words of Celtic bards, rather than being copied from books. The book is written in two volumes. The first contains material relating to the time of Merlin, then goes on to describe the future history of Britain. The second deals with more difficult material but includes prophecies about British history leading up to the 21st century. According to Merlin, the Apocalypse, or the end of the world, comes just after the 21st century. But what did Merlin have to say about the 20th century?

Merlin's Prophecies

Merlin talks about a long line of kings throughout history from the time of Vortigern and divides the time-line into three sections: the 6th–11th centuries, from the Saxons to the Normans; the 11th–17th centuries, which include a prophecy about the combining of the two kingdoms of Scotland and England under one king, which happened in 1603 under James VI of Scotland who became James I of England; and the 17th–21st centuries, which includes the present.

One passage in particular seems to lead into our era:

> All these things shall three ages see, till the buried kings shall be exposed to public view in the city of London.

This may well refer to the kings of England, buried at Westminster Abbey, becoming a tourist attraction open to public viewing. Another passage has a possible interpretation that is more sinister:

> In those days, the oaks of the forest shall burn, and acorns grow upon lime trees. The Severn Sea shall discharge itself through seven mouths, and the river Usk burn for seven months. Fishes shall die of the heat thereof, and from them serpents will be born.

The sea here is the Severn Estuary in the west of England – the site of a nuclear power station. The passage seems to indicate that there will be a terrible environmental disaster, including the mutation of plants and the death of animals.

One prophecy which may have already come true talks of the baths in the city of Bath. It says:

> The baths of Badon, or Bath, shall grow cold and their health-giving waters shall cause death.

Between 1979 and 1981, the hot springs of Bath, which are dedicated to the Roman goddess and prophetess Minerva, were declared to be polluted. Bathing and visits to the spring were stopped because the water was found to contain amebae that were supposedly the cause of one woman's death.

One more prophecy is worth mentioning. It describes a time when London is a wealthy city with underground trains and modern communications, and says:

> At that time shall the stones speak, and the area towards the Gallic coast shall be contracted by a narrow space.

It sounds as if Merlin was prophesying the coming of the Channel Tunnel, which is certainly a narrow space leading to the Gallic (which means "French") coast.

Much of Merlin's prophetic work is too steeped in ancient symbolism and imagery for us to understand properly. He used a lot of animal imagery, including lions, boars, and especially dragons. Perhaps one day more will be understood of what he prophesied.

CHAPTER 9

Nostradamus

The physician squinted up at the hot sun and wiped his brow. It was warm in Ancona and the road seemed to stretch ahead for ever. He trudged on, trying not to feel the heat. Minutes later he looked up to see a tiny smudge on the horizon. The smudge grew as he made his way along the road and soon swelled into the shapes of men. The physician was wary at first. They might be robbers, or worse. Then he relaxed, as he saw that the men were wearing the habits of Franciscan monks. They were unlikely to do him any harm.

When the Franciscans were no more than a few yards away, the physician stood aside to let them pass. Then suddenly, without warning, he threw himself on to the ground at the feet of one of the young monks. The startled monk stared down at the strange man kneeling before him and asked what on earth he was doing. The physician replied that he was kneeling before "His Holiness." The monk, whose name was Felix Peretti, was extremely embarrassed. He was nothing more than a former swineherd from a local village, hardly a "Holiness" of any sort. His companions were very much amused at such goings-on, and joked among themselves as they went on their way, leaving the physician still on his knees. They assumed that he was either drunk or mad, or perhaps the sun had got to him.

Of course, he was none of these things. The physician was Michel Nostradamus, the renowned prophet, and Father Peretti, the young monk, was destined to become Cardinal of Montalato, and in 1585, 19 years after the death of Nostradamus, he was elected as Pope Sixtus V!

The Healer

This is just one of the many stories of second-sight attributed to Nostradamus, the most famous of all prophets. Nostradamus was born Michel de Nostredame on December 14, 1503 in the small town of Rémy-en-Crue in Provence, France. His father was a Jew who had recently converted to Christianity, but he took little Christian interest in the boy and Michel was brought up by his grandfather, Jean de Rémy. Jean taught him Latin, Greek, Hebrew, medicine, and astrology. When Michel was ready, he was sent to study medicine at the university of Montpellier. He passed his exams without difficulty and was able to help when plague broke out in Provence. Michel had learned the value of good hygiene and fresh air, as well as of a good diet low in fat, to combat the dreaded disease. After four years he returned to Montpellier to receive his degree.

Two years later he began his travels again, this time settling in the town of Agen. Here, he became friends with the great scholar Scaliger, who may have taught him much about the "sciences" that the Church found so harmful. Anyone caught studying the arts of astrology or professing to possess second sight was condemned as a heretic and put to death!

In Agen he married and practiced medicine until the plague broke out again. It was an awful time and the plague killed both his wife and his children. He was devastated and, to make matters worse, he was hounded out of Agen, accused of heresy. There followed eight years of wandering, during which time he began to receive serious flashes of second-sight. It was then that his meeting with Peretti took place.

The Prophet

In 1546, Michel de Nostredame, now using the Latin name of Nostradamus, went to Aix-en-Provence, still fighting the horrors of the plague. We cannot imagine how terrible it must have been with unburied bodies lying in the streets and the constant stench of death. No one knew about germs at that time, so it was fortunate that Nostradamus knew the benefits of hygiene. He also concocted a pill, made from rose petals and other herbs, which patients were told to keep under their tongues until it dissolved. His treatment was so successful that he was granted a pension. From Aix he went to Salon, where he decided to settle. He married again, bought a house and spent the rest of his life there practicing medicine as well as making cosmetics.

Nostradamus also indulged his interest in the occult, and converted a room at the top of his house into a secret study. It was during this time that he began to write his prophecies. In fact, it was the night of Good Friday, 1554. He proposed to write the prophecies as ten volumes, or Centuries, of one hundred four-line poems called quatrains. The first three Centuries were published in May 1555. They open with a dedication to his son, Cesar. The dedication contained confessions and an outline of the techniques Nostradamus used to make his prophecies. It also contained a prose prophecy in which he "saw" as far as the year 3797. The final Centuries were completed by 1558, along with a letter containing another prose prophecy which is known as the Epistle to Henry II. This is a very strange vision that is difficult to understand, much like the biblical Book of Revelations.

A Royal Prophet

The quatrains were not written in any time order and most

are extremely hard to understand. Nostradamus was very aware of the Inquisition of the Catholic Church and did not want to be discovered and punished. So he had to make sure that his writings were mostly obscure. There are, however, some very clear passages, as we shall see.

In his opening dedication, he told his son that he burned all his books on magic in case they might be abused by those seeking power. He also described how he began to have visions that led to the prophecies in the quatrains. He described using a divining or scrying bowl filled with water and set upon a tripod in order to fix his attention and enter into a trance. He may also have used some sort of hallucinogenic drug in the bowl, the vapors of which he inhaled. Whatever method he used, though, the results were spectacular.

By 1556, he was all the rage in the French court and a particular favorite of the Queen, Catherine de Medici. In quatrain 35 of Century I, Nostradamus correctly predicted the death of her husband, Henry II, in a jousting accident. Henry died in 1559 when part of a jousting lance pierced his face-guard and entered his brain. The accident made Nostradamus even more famous, but at the same time it increased the number of Catholics who wanted to see him burned as a heretic. Things grew more dangerous for him in the 1560s when France became plagued with religious wars. However, the Duke and Duchess of Savoy became his patrons, or backers, and he was able to continue his work until he died in 1566. Needless to say, he predicted his own death with startling accuracy.

CHAPTER 10

The Prophecies of Nostradamus

The very strict rules of the Catholic Church and its hatred of those who did not obey them meant that Nostradamus had to disguise his prophecies carefully. But mostly he wanted to conceal their meaning from ignorant people who might selfishly want the future to correspond to their hopes and fears. Also, he was afraid that some evil tyrant might use the prophecies to recognize his own future mistakes in advance, take avoiding action and so succeed where he should have failed. For these reasons Nostradamus used many tricks to conceal the true meanings of the prophecies. Indeed, some are so difficult to decipher that we still do not know what they mean.

Nostradamus's quatrains contain many tricks of Latin grammar. For instance, he often used something called apheresis, which is the elimination of one or more letters or sounds from the beginning of a word. He also used apocope, which is the omission of the last sound or syllable of a word. Sometimes he added an extra letter or syllable to the beginning of a word, which is called prosthesis; or he shortened a word by dropping a sound or letter from the middle of it, which is called syncope. The interpreter of his poems has to pick up on all these tricks.

Anagrams were used as well, with phrases and words scrambled to make other words or phrases. For instance, "Paris," was turned into the new word "rapis," using the same letters. Sometimes Nostradamus used variations on anagrams by dropping or adding letters, just to make things even more difficult. For instance, *noir*, meaning "black" in French, can actually mean *roi*, or "king."

Many other tricks and red herrings were used as well, including animal names for countries, names hidden within normal words, and even the number of the quatrain relating to the date of the event it described.

There is no sequence of time in the Centuries, so one quatrain may talk of an event in 2010 while the next may describe an event in the 18th century. This made the quatrains seem like a jumble of meaningless poems. It may be that the prophecies came to Nostradamus in no particular order, and so that is how he wrote them down. Again, though, his object was to confuse the reader who is not on his wavelength.

The Future of France

Nevertheless, Nostradamus, with the help of his secretary, Jean-Aymes de Chavigny, knew that his gift had to be used, and so he set about composing the Centuries. In the preface, the letter to his baby son, he said, "I was willing to pass over what might be harmful ..." then changed his mind, adding "Then I thought I would enlarge a little, touching the Vulgar Advent, and show by obstruse and twisted sentences the future causes." In other words, he felt he had to give people a chance to see what might happen – no doubt in order that they might learn from what they saw.

The Vulgar Advent that he mentioned in the preface was the French Revolution, then about 200 years in the future, and he had much to say about it. But were his prophecies close to the mark, or even spot on? Here are two examples:

> Before the war, the great wall will fall
> The king will be executed, his death very sudden, and lamented.
> The masses will swim in blood
> And near the Seine, the soil will be bloodstained.
> Century 2, quatrain 57

This quatrain refers to the storming of the Bastille, a famous event at the start of the Revolution or "the war." The masses had assembled at the Bastille, a fortified prison near the River Seine, simply to demonstrate. But the walls were so poorly defended that they soon fell. The governor of the Bastille, De Launey (the "king" in the poem), was murdered by the bloodthirsty mob.

The second example referred to the French King, Louis XVI, and his wife Marie Antoinette, as they tried to escape the country in 1791.

> By night there will come by the forest of Reines
> A married couple by a devious route.
> A Queen – white stone, a monk – king in gray at Varennes.
> Elected Capet, causes tempest, fire, and bloody slicing.
> Century 9, quatrain 20

When the King and Marie Antoinette fled from the Tuileries in Paris, their road took them through the forest of Varennes. But their coach-driver lost his way and they had to take a different, or devious, route. The "Queen" in the third line refers to Marie Antoinette, who was wearing white on the night of the escape. King Louis was wearing gray when he reached Varennes. Louis's last name, the royal name, was Capet. And he did indeed bring about tempest and fire, but especially bloody slicing. The dreaded guillotine of the French Revolution sliced off many a head, including his own!

These two quatrains are among Nostradamus's most brilliant prophecies. And in the second he did far better than coming close to the mark – he was spot on.

We know that Nostradamus used astrological computations to help with his prophecies, especially with regard to dates. He was not always correct in dating events, but in the "king's escape" quatrain he was again totally accurate. Often, he used the numbers of the Century and the quatrain to display the date of the event he was writing about. The number of the "escape" quatrain is 20 – the date of the "escape" was June 20, 1791!

Another quatrain that uses its number to indicate a date brings us much closer to the present. It is quatrain 45 from Century 5.

> The great Empire will soon be desolated,
> And transferred near the forest of the Ardennes:
> The two illegitimate ones will be beheaded by the oldest,
> Aenobarbus will rule, the hawk-nosed one.
> Century 5, quatrain 45

During the battles in France in World War II, the Germans noticed that the French defences were very weak on a particular approach to the Ardennes forest. The French did not think a heavily-armored enemy division would try to get through the forest to attack them. However, they were wrong, and the Germans broke through to defeat the

French and rule France. That was in 1940. Five years later, the Ardennes was the scene of a major setback for the Germans at the Battle of the Bulge. Within months, the Nazi Empire was destroyed.

This quatrain refers to two events happening in one place. The first "Empire" is France, which was desolated by the German armies. The second is Germany herself. "Aenobarbus" probably refers to Adolf Hitler, while "the hawk-nosed one" is, no doubt, Charles de Gaulle, the French tank commander and later head of France, whose nose was seriously hooked.

But it is the date of the second event that is really interesting. The end of the war occurred in 1945, and the number of the quatrain is 45! Also, the total destruction of the Nazi Empire happened in May of that year, the fifth month, which corresponds to the number of the Century.

Today as Viewed from the 15th Century

So far, we know that Nostradamus did very well prophesying about events that happened in our past. But what about today? Has he been successful in seeing our present and, if so, what has he seen?

One of man's greatest adventures in the 20th century has been the exploration of space. And it would seem odd if Nostradamus did not see anything relating to it. In fact, he saw more than one event, although one quatrain in particular seems especially clear because it involves a disaster. And Nostradamus often locked into disasters – perhaps as a warning to those who might become involved.

> Nine shall be isolated from the rest of humanity,
> Isolated from judgement and advice.
> Their fate will be sealed from the moment of departure.
> Kappa, Theta, and Lambda dead, gone, scattered.
> Century 1, quatrain 81

In general, the quatrain prophesies the Challenger disaster of January 28, 1986, when the crew of the 25th Challenger mission was killed in an explosion one minute after take-off. Nostradamus got the number of astronauts wrong – there were seven – but they were certainly isolated from humanity, locked away in their space capsule. Also, their fate was sealed before departure, because the fault was already in the system. Can you imagine how Nostradamus must have felt seeing this vision? Later it was revealed that there had been some incorrect decision-making by the Space Administration command, which would certainly have created an incident "isolated from judgement and advice." The final line is composed of the names of Greek letters and may be an anagram of the rocket manufacturer, Morton Thiokol. After the disaster, many company heads were fired – banished and scattered.

Desert Storm

Nostradamus was very concerned about what might happen in the Middle East at the end of the 20th century. He certainly saw much conflict and hatred there, a vision that we see on our television screens whenever the Israeli-Palestinian disputes are shown. We also saw a complete war, from beginning to end, when Saddam Hussein of Iraq invaded Kuwait. This is what the great prophet had to say about it:

> The Europeans will come:
> Americans accompanied by the British and others.
> They will lead a great military force, colored and white,
> And go against the leader of Iraq.
> Century 10, quatrain 86

Saddam Hussein and his armies invaded the small Arab country of Kuwait on August 2, 1990. Kuwait is a vital oil supplier to Western countries, so within a week the West had reacted. American and British forces began to assemble in neighboring Saudi Arabia. European forces followed, and a counter-attack against the Iraqis was launched. It was called Operation Desert Storm. Soldiers, both black and white, fought against Saddam who prophesied that he would unleash "a holocaust against the alliance in the Mother of Battles." Saddam had not read his Nostradamus. In just seven days Saddam's armies were routed! Again, you can only wonder at what Nostradamus must have thought if he had a vision of the mighty tanks crossing the desert.

Nostradamus also prophesied about events after our time, and we shall look at some of these prophecies in Chapter Fifteen.

CHAPTER 11

The Hitler Prophecy

Karl Ernst Krafft was born in 1900. He was a gifted astrologer who, among other things, tried to prove that astrology worked by studying thousands of horoscopes of famous men, then demonstrating that the major events in their lives and their exact dates of death could be predicted from their natal, or birth, horoscopes. In 1939 he produced a huge book, crammed with statistics, called *Treatise on Astro-Biology*. It was not taken seriously. However, on November 2, 1939, he sent a letter to a Nazi Intelligence chief in which he predicted that Hitler's life would be in danger from an explosive between November 7 and 10.

On November 8, 1939, there was a bomb attempt on Hitler's life in the Bürgerbräu beer hall in Munich, Germany. It killed 7 people and wounded 63. Hitler escaped unhurt.

Krafft later became a victim of the Nazis. Hitler did not

like astrologers and got rid of as many as he could. Krafft died on his way to Buchenwald in 1945.

The Cayce Case

Edgar Cayce was a famous American clairvoyant and healer who was born on a farm near Hopkinsville, Kentucky, in 1877. As a child his gifts were not taken seriously and were considered no more than the result of an over-active imagination. He did impress with his learning ability, though, which often involved sleeping with his school books under his head. Later he was able to cure himself of a paralysis of the throat muscles by going into a trance and learning for himself what his medication and therapy should be.

Soon, local doctors were using him to diagnose their patients and his fame grew. Sometimes he could diagnose an ailment merely by knowing where the patient was. He did it apparently through telepathy of some sort. In all, is thought to have cured over 14,000 people!

Cayce was not just a healer, though. He was a prophet. And his prophecies seem to deal mostly with physical changes to the planet. For instance, he prophesied that new lands would appear in the Atlantic and the Pacific. One of these "islands," he said, would be part of the submerged continent of Atlantis. Apparently, in 1974, archaeologists found part of this island off the coast of the Bimini Islands in the Bahamas, exactly where Cayce had said it would be.

He also predicted that the Great Lakes in Canada would one day empty south into the Gulf of Mexico. This would be a total reversal of the present circumstances because the Lakes currently empty north into the Atlantic. The southern route would take the waters through the Mississippi Valley and into the Gulf of Mexico. This brings up one of Cayce's other prophecies – that soon there will be a frightening world food shortage. If the Great Lakes prophecy comes true, a huge food-growing area of the United states will be lost.

Cayce's main prophecies involve the break-up of the Earth's crust and the resulting destruction to the land and those who live on it. He saw the changes happening when conditions in the South Pacific, as well as those in the Etna region of the Mediterranean, began to alter. The South Pacific break-up is probably the large "subduction" zone, where the western boundary of the Pacific tectonic plate (the continental plate that forms part of the Earth's crust) pushes itself down and under the Indo-Australian plate. The Earth's crust is made up of moving plates which either push into one another or pull apart from one another. When the plate edge sinks it causes areas of stress, which are marked by earthquake activity and volcanoes. The area in the South Pacific is called the Ring of Fire because of the many volcanoes there, and certainly there is a chance that great changes could be seen in this area. Luckily Cayce's prophecies have not yet come true, although that area and others are always being watched for activity.

Cayce also prophesied that a huge part of the islands of Japan would sink into the Pacific, again as a result of plate movement. In the United States he thought that the North East would be affected, and if there was activity in the South Pacific, then the coast of California would experience the effects. We know that in this area lies the unstable San Andreas fault. And there have been many earthquakes around it, some of which have damaged cities in Southern California. It is here that scientists think the next really big earthquake will take place. Perhaps Cayce knew more than he was saying. Or perhaps he was just a good geologist. We shall have to wait and see!

The Doom Prophets

Although Nostradamus and others prophesied that the world would go through turbulent times in the future, they also had many positive things to say. Some prophets, however, see only doom and gloom for all of us.

In 1886 a man called C.T. Russell wrote a book called *The Divine Plan of the Ages.* In it he tried to show how God was planning to end the world in a very short while. Russell explained that, in the time left, we must follow God's higher purpose and be aware of His plan in creating the world in the way He has. The book sold six million copies in several languages. Russell felt that it was his job to show everyone the light and the true way. Some modern organizations still take what he had to say seriously, and still meet to await the day of doom.

Another messenger of doom was Elizabeth Clare Prophet, who reckoned she was in contact with all the great religious leaders of the past. She predicted, on the basis of her "cosmic clock," a world catastrophe in 1990. Because of her warning, thousands of her followers sold their houses and moved out of the cities. Needless to say, most now wish they hadn't.

These two examples are quite different to that of Edgar Cayce. He certainly had some form of gift which allowed him to reach a higher consciousness. His ability as a healer was there for all to see, and he refused to take money for what he did. Whether he was as successful in his prophecies has yet to be proven.

The Tibetan Connection

Helena Petrovna Blavatsky was born the daughter of a Russian colonel in 1831. She had a very charismatic personality and married at the age of 16. When that relationship failed she began her travels around the world. Madame Blavatsky, as she came to be known, soon developed a reputation as a medium. Her power, she said, came from certain monks in far-off Tibet, and was relayed to her through telepathy. These monks were spiritual masters and included a Tibetan entity called Djwhal Khul.

An Englishwoman called Alice Bailey did not have Madame Blavatsky's outgoing personality. However, like her, she was contacted through telepathic channels by Djwhal Khul, who became known as "The Tibetan." Khul, who was the head of a lamasery in Shigatse, Tibet, sent her enough "wisdom" to fill 19 books. The wisdom was *The*

Secret Doctrine of the Tibetan monks, which had been passed on for thousands of years in that Himalayan country. The basic idea of this doctrine is that behind all the realities of our world is a higher, divine reality that we cannot fully understand. Only a few gifted people, such as prophets, gain a first-hand knowledge of this reality. This seems to be another way of saying that prophets tap into a higher consciousness, which we know already.

Among the many things relayed to Alice Bailey through the telepathic link were prophecies. These prophecies cover events that have occurred in the past as well as those that will occur over the next million years. They tell of the coming of the atomic age and the astrological Age of Aquarius, as well as a time when all religions will follow the same basic principles.

According to Djwhal Khul, the Age of Aquarius will be a pretty amazing time. Racism will end, people will live in a brotherly fashion, and healing will be a major factor. Strange as it may seem, Russia will play a big role in the new age of humanity. During the last years of the 1990s the great Chinese philosopher Confucius will be reincarnated to lead the work of building the new age of brotherhood. Towards the year 1999, the forces of evil will come together, which will cause problems for those setting up the New Age. Somehow there will be a destruction of the old way of life and a more positive one will emerge at the end of the century. This sounds again like the prophecy of world conflict in the late 1990s. At the beginning of the next century there will be a redistribution of resources, so no one nation should suffer poverty. Political changes will be made as well. This will lead to a world federation, or union, of nations. Some time before 2245, the Second Coming of Jesus will occur. He will work as the head of a religious group, and will lead mankind to the Mount of Ascension. This should mean the end of strife for all of humanity.

So far, the prophecies of Djwhal Khul have been fairly accurate. But it remains to be seen what will happen in the next century. What we do know is that the next century and the new Millennium should be very special if the major prophets are correct in their predictions.

CHAPTER 12

Revelations

Many prophets speak with some authority about the end of the world, when it will happen, and how. It is all part of the "from creation to destruction" aspect of prophecy that sees time as having a beginning and an end. The prophet uses his ability to reach a higher consciousness, as a means of tapping into the time-frame at different points. For instance, the Book of Revelations, in the New Testament of the Christian Bible, tells us about the end of the world and what will happen. It is not a pretty sight for sinners, with all the trappings of a good, old-fashioned horror movie!

Revelations was written by St. John the Divine, at a place called Patmos, a Greek island in the Aegean Sea. Revelations describes the final years of the world and the redemption, or salvation, of mankind. The writings of the Old Testament prophets brought us up to the birth of

Jesus. That year is the central point in the Christian idea of time. The years before that time are designated BC (which means "before Christ"), while the years after are AD or Anno Domini, which means "in the year of our Lord." After the birth of Jesus, Revelations states that 3,000 more years will pass before the Christian period comes to an end. Revelations tells us what is to happen and John made sure that Christians took him seriously:

> Blessed is he that readeth, and they that hear the words of this prophecy, and keep those things that are written herein; for the time is at hand.

This is a warning to pay attention. The prophecy told of the Second Coming of Christ, and warned what would happen to those who did not take heed. Revelations is full of weird images and creatures, yet they are not the usual Christian ones. This is because the prophecy probably drew on other ancient mystery cults from Greece, Asia, and the Middle East to provide it with meaning.

The Vision

St. John the Divine saw a huge throne surrounded by 24 elders dressed in white, wearing gold crowns. All around was thunder and lightning. Seven lamps burned, giving off light for the "Holy One" who held a scroll, or book, with seven seals. No man or woman was worthy of opening the seals. Then a lamb with seven horns and seven eyes appeared. It represented Jesus and Aries, the first sign of the zodiac. The lamb took the book and opened the first four

100 • **Prophecies**

seals. The famous Four Horsemen of the Apocalypse then appeared. The last horseman was Death riding on a pale horse. It was his job to kill with hunger and the sword.

When the sixth seal was opened, all those who had been killed in the name of God appeared. At this point a huge earthquake rocked the ground, the sun grew dark, and the moon turned bright red. The stars fell from the heavens and all the mountains and islands of the world shifted. This was the great day of God's anger. Then the angels of wind came and one sealed the foreheads of all those who would be saved on the Day of Judgement. There were only 144,000 – enough to fill Wembley stadium or the Toronto Superdome only a couple of times over!

With the seventh seal, peace came for a time, after which seven angels appeared and terrible catastrophes began to happen. A star called Wormwood fell from the sky, and this represented the acts of man against his creator, then horrible demons attacked everyone who had not had their foreheads sealed by the angel. Plagues came next – perhaps Aids – then locusts, scorpions, and other hideous creatures tormented those on earth until everyone prayed for death. Another star brought a book that John had to eat in order to digest its ancient wisdom. He was then told to prophesy to all peoples and to save those who have "given witness" and repented their sins.

A pregnant woman now appeared, wearing a crown of 12 stars. She was threatened by a red dragon with 10 horns and 7 heads. This is the Beast of the Apocalypse whose number is 666 and is called the Antichrist. More death and destruction followed. Finally, God intervened. A white horse appeared with the word of God upon it, followed by the armies of God clothed in white. The armies made war against the Beast and slew him.

Then the Book of Life was opened and everyone was judged according to what he or she had done. Those who did not come up to scratch were pitched into a lake of fire. Finally, a new heaven and earth were created and the grace of God was passed to everyone in the new world and the new city of Jerusalem.

The lesson to be learned from this nightmarish vision is fairly clear. If you obey the word of God you are rewarded. If you don't, you perish.

Some people take the prophecy literally, but most regard it as a symbolic work, which it surely is. There are many other end-of-the-world, or apocalyptic, writings that sound much like Revelations, and many of them come from the original New Testament. Others refer to other religious beliefs. Most are simply warnings that you will be punished if you don't behave. In that case, we have to look at the vision of Revelations as a symbolic guide, and not a horrible picture of some reality that will definitely happen in the future.

CHAPTER 13

Prophets from Other Cultures

Different cultures have different ways of searching for and reaching the realms of higher consciousness that allow prophecy to take place. There are the oracles of the Greeks, the scrying bowls of the Egyptians, and the shamans of Asia and Africa, to name a few. But one of the most interesting is the ancient Chinese method of divining that involves reading different configurations of written symbols. This method is contained in the famous I Ching, the Chinese Book of Changes.

The I Ching began as a sequence of 64 oracles written by King Wên, founder of the Chinese dynasty over 3,000 years ago. The oracles were later expanded upon with images and commentaries on individual lines. Many people, including Confucius, the great philosopher and scholar, wrote commentaries on all of the I Ching, which resulted in a large volume of work. The first English-language translation was published in 1949 and spanned two volumes.

The divining system is based on the simple opposites of light and darkness, or positive and negative, which the Chinese call yin and yang. Yin represents the dark, or "other side," of the mind. Yang, the positive and good.

Yang is represented by an unbroken line, like this:

———

Yin is represented by a broken line, like this:

—— ——

Each of the sixty-four oracles is made up of six of these lines, stacked on top of one another:

———
—— ——
———
—— ——
———
—— ——

The six lines represent what is called a hexagram, and each hexagram has a name. The one shown above is the twenty-first hexagram, called Shi He.

The sequence of hexagrams, plus the commentaries on them, can be used either as a guide to how to behave under different circumstances or as an oracle that tells what could happen in the future – a form of self-prophecy.

Using the I Ching

A PROPHECY

I was introduced to the I Ching many years ago but use it infrequently. On one occasion I interpreted a particular hexagram to mean that I should soon walk down the aisle of a church with a young bride at my side. I cannot remember what the original question was, but the hexagram didn't seem to make any sense at all. I chuckled. This time the I Ching had been caught out. I couldn't take any bride down the aisle because I was already married, and I intended to stay that way. Nor could I lead a daughter down the aisle because I didn't have any children.

I put it out of my mind and thought no more about it. Then, about a month later, I received a phone call from my sister who was studying at a university in Montreal. She was very excited, and took a while to get round to the reason for her phone call. Finally, she came out with it. She and her boyfriend had decided to get married as soon as possible – even though they were not officially engaged. My face went pale as I remembered the prophecy of the I Ching. My father had died when I was 16. It would therefore be my job, as the oldest male in the family, to give away the bride. That meant that I would certainly walk down the aisle of a church with a bride on my arm, exactly as the I Ching had predicted.

Native Americans

The natives of both North and South America have a long history of prophecy, much of it part of their sequence of myths and legends. The Mayan civilization is usually thought to be part of the drift of Asian peoples south through the Americas. They crossed to what is now Alaska via a land-bridge. The bridge became covered with water thousands of years ago and is now the Bering Strait.

Another suggestion, which was confirmed by Edgar Cayce in a vision, is that the Mayas were relics of the ancient civilization of Atlantis. Whatever the truth, they had an extraordinary interest in time and developed two yearly calendars, one of which is based on a year of 365.242129 days, which is thought to be more accurate than our own Gregorian calendar! The other year, used for religious purposes, has only 260 days. This calendar holds the Mayan great prophecy for the future. But we will talk about that later on.

Quetzalcoatl's Prophecy

The Mayas also had many myths, and the most important character in Mayan myth is Quetzalcoatl. His name comes from the quetzal bird, which is a magnificent creature with red and green feathers. The story of Quetzalcoatl, the pale, bearded priest-king, begins with his birth in AD 947. He grew up to become a great ruler, and introduced fasting and confession to his people as well as the true arts of civilization. His sacred center of Tula became the capital city of the Mayan Empire.

But nothing lasts forever, and in time Quetzalcoatl's brother, Tezcatlipoca, connived to bring down his brother. This he did by lacing his brother's drink with the juice of a magic mushroom and making him drunk. When Quetzalcoatl awoke after a night of carousing he was so filled with remorse that he abdicated his throne and went into exile. As he left, though, he prophesied that he would return and bring a new order, and at the same time the people of Tula would suffer calamities and persecution. He said that he would return from the east, like the morning star at the beginning of the nine hells cycle of the Mayan calendar.

On Good Friday, April 25, 1519, a pale, bearded man arrived from the east. But to the Maya, and to the Aztecs and their king Montezuma II, it was not Good Friday but the first day of the nine hells cycle – the prophesied date of Quetzalcoatl's return. The calamities and persecutions were soon to begin, with the roar of cannon, and the screams of death and disease. The pale, bearded one was the Spanish conquistador, Cortés, making good use of Quetzalcoatl's prophecy. Montezuma was murdered and the Aztec and other empires destroyed. Within a period of about 50 years, a population of 25 million Native Americans in the central part of America was reduced to less than 1 million.

CHAPTER 14

Being a Prophet

We have looked at prophets and their prophecies, many of which have come true. But what of the future? What has been prophesied for the new Millennium and beyond? Many prophets have described their visions of it, and we'll be looking at those. But perhaps we should also see what we can do for ourselves. We all have the potential to reach that higher consciousness, but how do we go about becoming a prophet?

Being a prophet is not much like other occupations. You can't go down to the unemployment office and ask the person behind the desk if they have any work for prophets today. Some people are inspired to prophesy and some are not. There are some things you can do, though, to help inspiration come along.

Long ago our primitive ancestors knew of and interacted

with the unseen forces of the world and the universe. The ancient Peruvians called these forces and energies *huaca*. The native North American peoples called them the *orenda* or spirit forces. Their more open and expansive consciousness allowed them to plug into these sources of energy. Over the years, as man has developed his intelligence and his ability to reason, he has in some ways blunted his consciousness, so he has become less able to tap into the unseen energies in the way he once did. Some people still know how to do this – and among these people are the prophets. This doesn't mean that only gifted prophets and the like can tune into the universe. In fact, we can all use these energies and forces if we try. We can all attempt to be prophets. Some may achieve brilliant results, others may not. The secret is to use what is there and hidden from us in everyday life.

First of all, we must open our minds to the vast expanse of possibilities, and not be hemmed in by the merely materialistic. We must look inwards as often as we normally look outwards. There are various ways we can do this, and they are what the prophets do to open up their minds to altered, or expanded, consciousness. We can meditate, recall our dreams, or even shift into a trance. Who knows what might be achieved? Best of all, once that energy has been tapped and the mind can see beyond the material limits of the world, there is no longer such a condition as boredom. Prophets simply don't get bored. They know there is no limit to what they can achieve!

Waves and Prophets

No one can know exactly how these unseen forces and

energies work. Some say there is no scientific basis for prophecy or other occult phenomena. But consider this. Scientists will tell us that the building blocks of energy and matter are waves. A wave consists of two halves, and is measured from the top of the bump to the bottom of the next trough. Light is composed of waves of one length, sound consists of waves of a different length, and so on. Cosmic radiation is made up of very fast waves, and there is cosmic radiation throughout the universe. Perhaps it is his or her ability to lock into certain cosmic wave patterns that allows the prophet to know what the future may hold. Perhaps time itself is a sort of wave pattern, and this energy allows the prophet to step outside what we experience as time and to move through parallel time zones. It's not such a wild notion. After all, the minds of our great-great-grandparents would have boggled at the idea of the Internet! We need to believe in possibilities outside our own rather small environment full of everyday things, if we are to achieve something really worthwhile. We must get beyond Game Boy and Playstation.

Easing the Mind

Meditation is a great way to ease the mind and relax the body. And the best meditation pose to aid energy-flow is the hunter's posture, which involves sitting cross-legged on the ground. One of the main Celtic images of this pose is the god Cernunnos, who was closely associated with prophecy. Sitting this way helps the body to tune into the Earth. And prophetic tradition often works through underground forces that are associated with the land. Another useful posture is to sit with your head between your legs so your body makes a closed circle. This creates a circuit of vital energies.

Once in position, it is best to observe a period of silence. This allows all your impulses and emotions to remain still while you wait for the spiritual voice within to speak to you.

Learning Myths

Often we do not understand the ancient prophecies because we do not understand the images that they use, all of which come from ancient mythic traditions. These traditions of story-telling, often in verse, are part of the fabric of our humanity. They help to make us what we are. Prophecy is directly connected with creation myths, and many prophetic words and visions come from these myths. So it's worth reading about them as much as possible. They will enlighten you and open the door to a higher understanding of societies both old and new. And they will put you in the right spiritual frame of mind for prophecy.

Systems

It's always best to follow one system, and usually the simpler the better. Nostradamus had his bowl of water and nothing could be more simple than that, yet it worked for him. One thing is certain, though – real prophecy does not come through drugs. All you need is something to focus on, something to arouse the energy and the power within you.

Fasting and Cleansing

Fasting has to do with purification and good health. Its

main aim, along with other purifying acts such as bathing or having a sauna, is to cleanse the body, and in particular the blood, of toxins, which are substances the body does not tolerate. Prophecy seems to involve a close link between the bloodstream and vital energy.

If you are unhealthy, which usually means being overweight or full of toxins, your vital energy levels are probably low. Fasting can get rid of the toxins and help you to lose weight which, in turn, builds up your vital energy levels. It is important, though, not to take fasting to excess. The most important thing is to be healthy, and to build up your vital energy. You will also have more vital energy if you eat a healthy, well-balanced diet, with plenty of fresh fruit and vegetables, and take regular exercise.

The Environment

Prophecy often involves working with the things around us. Myths about the land and the stars can all play their part in helping us to reach a higher consciousness. So it is wise to be aware of the cycles of the seasons and the planets. Prophets sometimes meditate in particular places, or at particular times, which they feel are power-centers. It may be at a full moon or when Venus is in a particular relationship to a star pattern. Whenever it is, it can help you to meditate and concentrate. Finding a particular place also helps, as Merlin discovered when he went into his cave. Prophecy is often linked with the darker forces of the underworld, which sometimes appear as steam coming from the Earth, as is the case with the sibyl at Delphi. Wherever you choose, though, will be your own choice and will feel right to you.

Perhaps soon you will join with Nostradamus and others in prophesying what will occur at and after the Millennium. Whatever happens, it is bound to be an interesting time.

The Millennium

At the present time, when we think of the future, we inevitably think of the Millennium. The Millennium may mean simply the beginning of the next thousand years, or it may mean the Second Coming of Jesus. To some, it even means the coming of a new age – the Age of Aquarius. This is the next age in the great astrological "year" which takes 25,826 years to complete and is based on the spinning of our planet in relation to the 12 astrological constellations.

The Millennium may also mean the beginning of the last thousand years in a cycle of seven, and the last cycle before the end of the world as we know it. We don't yet know but, whatever it means, it is important, and it is the period that has created the most prophetic activity, both modern and ancient. It is now time to look at the Millennium prophecies and see exactly what the prophets believe is in store for us!

CHAPTER 15

The Millennium Prophecies

The Middle East seems to figure prominently in the story of prophecy, with the Babylonians at the head. Even they had something to say about the Millennium.

The Babylonian Cycle

King Sargon of Akkad compiled a multi-volume astronomical work called the *Illumination of Bel*. Bel was a god. In that work, prophets predicted that "when all the planets meet in the constellation of Capricorn the world will be destroyed by fire." This astrological meeting or conjunction occurs once every 25,826 years. Six of the nine planets in our Solar System met in Capricorn on January 15, 1991. There was also a powerful solar eclipse. But what else happened on that day? Believe it or not, it was the deadline that the United Nations had set for Iraq's withdrawal from

Kuwait. Iraq did not withdraw, so it was the start of the Gulf War, and potentially the beginning of the biggest global fire of all time if nuclear bombs had been used. This event, happening so close to the Millennium, would have been pretty much the end of the world if the worst had happened. Luckily, we seem to have avoided that catastrophe.

The Great Pyramid

The passageways and chambers of Egypt's Great Pyramid chart the passage of time from a beginning to an end. It is projected that the end of the pyramid's recorded time falls between July 1992 and September 2001. Projecting onwards, however, it is prophesied that a Kingdom of the Spirit will form between 1995 and 2025, which will value higher goals and ethics. However, physical catastrophes such as earthquakes and storms will become commonplace. Civilization will finally end after 2025 and a new order will be born. The reincarnation of Jesus will take place in 2040.

He will reincarnate twice more. The last date indicated in the Great Pyramid is 2979. Could that be the end of the world?

The Final Date

The final date given us directly by the Great Pyramid is September 17, 2001 – a pretty exact date. An astrological charting of this day shows that this may be the date on which there are magnetic changes in our relationship with the Sun. This shadows the polar shift theory, which is explained later in this chapter. Particular astrological signs point to a change of the Earth's position in relation to the Sun, which would certainly occur if the poles shifted.

Other signs show the linking of heaven and earth and the opening up of a higher consciousness in all of us. Somewhere along the line, it seems, the human race will undergo a change that alters our consciousness. This sounds like a kind of mutation, or a physical change in the brain. It might be due to the incoming radiation and other events linked to the changes in electromagnetic energy. Perhaps we are going to take another jump along the evolutionary trail. It sounds rather like Arthur C. Clark's *2001, A Space Odyssey*. Now, what was that date?

Jubilee

The number seven is sacred to the Hebrews and they divide up time into sequences of seven or multiples of it. There are seven days of the week. There is a Sabbath each week and a Sabbath each seven years. And every fiftieth year, or 7 × 7 + 1 year, is a jubilee. The last jubilee cycle was seven cycles of seven thousand years, then a jubilee period of one thousand years. The year 2000 sees the beginning of the jubilee Millennium, and it is prophesied that evil will end and a Utopia, like a heaven, will follow. This is a nicely positive prophecy, unlike the following prediction.

The Ten-horned Beast

In the Revelations of St. John the Divine, we come across a particularly gruesome beast with seven heads and ten horns. Notice the number seven again. Many people think these horns represent ten countries in some sort of alliance, and that it may be headed by what St. John and Nostradamus both call the Antichrist. Nostradamus wrote that three Antichrists would appear between his death and the Millennium. The first two are recognizable as Napoleon and Adolf Hitler. The third is about to arrive on the world scene. According to St. John, he will appear as a savior to mankind, but will soon show his true colors and turn to evil and the domination of our world. This is one of a number of prophecies that tell of the coming of someone powerful but evil around the time of the Millennium. One more thing – he is supposed to come from the Middle East. Could he already be among us?

The Mayan Prophecies

The Mayan calendar, as we have said, holds the key to a major prophecy about the future, and particularly about the Millennium. The Mayans calculated that the present cycle of history will end in 2012. The cycle began on July 26, 1992. These 20 years deal with some sort of time-shift, perhaps even a speeding-up of time. This will produce an increase in the vibration of matter and lead to a closer link with the spiritual world. Things will begin to come together in greater harmony, and a higher consciousness will be easier to attain. By the year 2012 we will have reached real harmony and made some form of breakthrough that will make us more aware of Nature and the nature of things while being less dependent on the materialist outlook that dominates our lives now. It will be as if the ancient wisdoms have returned and a new cycle has begun.

Polar Shift

Over a period of millions of years many catastrophes have befallen our poor planet, including the asteroid impact that probably triggered the end of the dinosaurs. Some people think that a number of these catastrophes can be linked to shifts in the Earth's magnetic poles. The magnetic poles are near the Earth's axis poles and mark the electromagnetic forces that wrap around the planet. In other words, the

Earth acts just like a big bar-magnet with a north pole at one end and a south pole at the other.

The polar shift theory suggests that, every now and then, the north magnetic pole changes places with the south, reversing the flow of electromagnetic force. As you might imagine, this would create terrible upheavals along the Earth's crust, producing earthquakes and volcanoes in abundance, not to mention atmospheric storms. It might also mean that the electromagnetic force stops flowing for a very short time. This would allow space debris such as meteorites to penetrate the atmosphere and hit the Earth, something the electromagnetic force normally prevents.

The last polar shift was apparently about 12,400 years ago. The next, it is thought, is imminent, maybe at the beginning of the Millennium! If this is so, it could account for the prophets' visions of earthquakes, storms, and general chaos, as well as the "stars" falling from the sky, Nostradamus's hailstones as big as eggs. The hailstones may be visions of falling meteorites.

But this is not something we should worry about. Oh, no! The prophets of polar shift say it is simply a way of cleansing the Earth and that things will be much better afterwards.

Let's hope so.

Nostradamus and the Millennium

Of all the prophets, it is clear that Nostradamus has the most extraordinary track record for getting things right. But he was not finished when he prophesied events for the 20th century. He also had the Millennium to deal with.

Let's see exactly what he prophesied for the Millennium and take note of it, because in the months to come it could be proved all over again that he was the greatest prophet we have ever known.

We have so far been able to link Nostradamus's prophecies with events that have happened since his death. But now we cannot do that. Now we have to interpret what he has to say for ourselves. And your interpretation may be as good as anyone else's. Some of his predictions may be more obvious than others, but here is a chance to test your interpretative skills.

> To the port of Agde, the ships will enter
> Carrying the infection of the pestilence, not the faith.
> Passing the bridge, a thousand thousand will be taken.
> And the bridge broken by the resistance of the third one.
> Century 8, quatrain 21

Most commentators think this quatrain is a clear reference to Aids because it talks of infection and the pestilence, or plague. But I think there is another interpretation.

Perhaps the ships entering refers to a western navy of some sort, which carries weapons or, at worst, the seeds of germ-warfare. Passing the bridge takes them into the East, perhaps Constantinople, the old Byzantium. During this time thousands are lost in battle and the bridge is broken by the resistance of the enemy led by the third one, in this case the third Antichrist. It is the reference to the third one that may be the key here. What do you think?

More Pestilence

> When the sacred temples have been plundered
> The greatest of lands profaning holy things.
> Because of their actions, an enormous pestilence will arrive.
> The King will not condemn them for their actions.
> Century 8, quatrain 62

Nostradamus seems obsessed with pestilence, which he thought was God's divine punishment for mankind. In this quatrain, the "greatest of lands" may refer to the United States, or possibly even to the Holy Land, where the greatest pestilences have been war and terrorism. Also, the line about "profaning holy things" may indicate a holy place where the "things" are to be found. Nevertheless, in the last line it seems as if the Lord will forgive everyone in the end, once the punishment has run its course.

But if the "King" refers to someone else, who could it be? And what then might the quatrain mean?

Famine

> The great famine which will visit the Earth,
> Will be spasmodic and then become universal.
> It will be so complete and long-lasting that people will harvest
> Roots from the woods and the child from the mother.
> Century 1, quatrain 67

The main gist of this quatrain is fairly obvious. It looks as if we are in for a big famine, one that starts gradually and then gets worse. Perhaps we have already seen the beginning of it with the terrible famines in Ethiopia, in which case we are talking about Third World famine. It will be so bad that people will have to dig roots to survive and no children will be born. Perhaps there is a hint that world agriculture will break down, although that would probably be caused by a nuclear holocaust. Or would it? Look at the number of people who are born into our world – 250,000 every day. The world population now is greater than 5.7 billion. In 20 years it will be over 8 billion. We live in a consume-and-waste society that uses up energy at an ever-increasing rate. The United States, the consumer paradise, uses one-quarter of the world's energy alone. By 2030, the population of China could eat up all of the world's grain produce. So, perhaps, as ever, Nostradamus is warning us. If we continue in the way we are going, great famine will indeed hit the Earth.

Earthquake

When the sun is in twenty degrees of Taurus, there will be a terrible earthquake.
The city full of people will be shattered.
The air, heaven, and earth will be shrouded in darkness,
When the infidel ignores God and the saints.
Century 9, quatrain 83

Nostradamus begins the quatrain by telling us on which day the earthquake will happen. It is May 10, the day on which the sun reaches 20° in the sign of Taurus. But, again, there is no year. The city in this case is most likely Los Angeles, although San Francisco is another candidate for being ignorant of "God and the saints" – in other words, ungodly. The darkening of the skies probably refers to the result of dust from the earthquake, or perhaps volcanic action that might accompany it.

The reference to an infidel is interesting. It may mean a city that is not Christian but which follows another religion. If this is the case, and we know where earthquake activity is likely to take place around the world, what other city might the quatrain refer to?

Volcanic Eruption

Earth shaking and fire from the center of the earth
Will cause the towers of the New City to shake.
Two great rocks will war for a long time
And Arethusa will cover the new river red.

Century 1, quatrain 87

It seems fairly clear that this quatrain refers to a volcanic eruption, and a pretty big one at that. But its location is something of a mystery. The New City is most likely a reference to New York, yet New York is not noted for its volcanic activity. The New River in that case would be the Hudson. The great rocks could refer to two tectonic plates that are pushing or grinding against each other. The volcano could therefore be Mount Etna in Sicily, Mount Pelée on Martinique, or Vesuvius in southern Italy. It could also be Mount Rainier in Washington State on the west coast of the United States. In that case, it would wipe out the new city of Tacoma in Washington.

"Earth shaking" could be a play on the nickname of Neptune, which is Earthshaker. That would indicate a tsunami, which is a massive ocean wave caused by an underwater volcanic eruption. Arethusa is a nymph from Greek mythology who turned herself into a spring. Turning herself red would indicate a flow of lava accompanying earthquakes and volcanic action.

ETs

Near Auch, Lectoure and Mirande,
A great fire from heaven for three nights will fall.
The cause will be seen as both amazing and miraculous.
Afterwards the Earth will tremble.
Century 1, quatrain 46

This is one of the quatrains in which Nostradamus may be telling us of a visit from ETs or extraterrestrials. The "great fire from heaven" may be a UFO coming in to land. It either takes a long time to do so or there is more than one of them. The landing of people from another planet would certainly be seen as amazing and miraculous. Note that Nostradamus does not say that it is a miracle. Afterwards the Earth may well tremble, either in fear or in delight.

One argument against extraterrestrial life visiting us is the extreme distances they would have to travel to get here. It would take hundreds or even thousands of years to cross the void between stars if the fastest you can travel is the speed of light. So who would bother to come? Perhaps someone who lives much longer than we do.

And what about the place names? That's for you to figure out!

The Apocalypse

In the year 1999, and seven months after,
From the sky will come the great King of Terror.
Resuscitating the great king of the Mongols
Before which Mars will reign in peace.

Century 9, quatrain 72

This quatrain is interpreted by many to be the quatrain of the Apocalypse, or the end of the world. So the end of the world will be in 1999. The King of Terror is thought to be Mabus, which is a distortion of the Latin word *malus*, meaning the evil one. This could be the third Antichrist whose arrival was predicted by Nostradamus, or it could be an extraterrestrial. The idea that he comes from the sky may not mean space, though. It may refer to a nuclear attack from the sky. The "great king of the Mongols" whose spirit is resuscitated, or revived, probably refers to Ghengis Khan, who was noted for war and conquest, not to mention pillage. This means the third Antichrist will emerge from the East.

Nostradamus's Warning

We have now seen a little of what Nostradamus thinks is in store for us, if his visions have been correctly interpreted. But we must remember that Nostradamus was not prophesying simply to tell us what will be. He was also giving us a warning. There are many possible futures, and we can choose our destiny. If we continue in the way we are heading, then Nostradamus's worst fears may be realized. If we heed his message and try to live in harmony with ourselves and Nature, then other, more positive, prophecies may come true, especially the ones predicting a more spiritual age. In the end, it's up to all of us.

New code, bright future

Not long ago, a new book was published which told of a brilliant new code. It was, the book said, embedded in the words of the Bible, and it was called 'The Bible Code.' The book, written by Dr. Jeffrey Satinover, and called *The Truth Behind the Bible Code*, was serialized in newspapers, and it caused great excitement. Could the Bible really hold the truth about what might happen in the future?

In fact, the Bible Code had been hinted at by Jewish scholars over the three thousand years since the traditional revelation of the Bible to Moses from Mount Sinai. But no one had been able to break the code or even discover how it worked. Since the Second World War, however, cryptology – the art of breaking and making codes – has been more or less perfected. And computers have been built that can cope with highly complex code-breaking.

It was a teacher of computer programming living in Israel, called Abrahan Oren, who started the ball rolling. He could see, and 'feel,' that certain patterns arose in the first books of the Old Testament, and that they seemed to occur more often than chance would allow. He went to work, and with the help of other mathemeticians, found names and groups of words encoded in the biblical verses that could not be there merely by chance. The code was broken, and it revealed many incredible things, including a view of our future.

Centuries ago, the mystical cabbalists told of a time when knowledge of the material world and of the spiritual world would "burst together like twin fountains," when knowledge of God and knowledge of science would work together. They predicted that it would happen at the end of the 6th millennium, and when the end of the Jewish exile had occurred. That means around the end of our millennium. Our knowledge of science has increased immeasurably over the past few years. Perhaps the decoding of the Bible is the beginning of a new spiritual understanding. If so, there is much to look forward to!